MW00398409

FUTURE SOCIAL

FUTURE SOCIAL

DESIGN IDEAS, ESSAYS AND DISCUSSIONS ON
SOCIAL HOUSING FOR THE 'HARDEST-TO-HOUSE'

BLUE*IM*PRINT

ACKNOWLEDGEMENTS

Future Social would not be possible without the help and support of numerous individuals and various organizations.

It owes its origin to the leadership of Professor Ray Cole as the then Director of the UBC School of Architecture and Landscape Architecture. The Province of British Columbia's Housing Endowment Fund enabled the project through generous funding while an array of BC Housing and Housing Policy Branch staff contributed to its success. Particular gratitude goes to Jodi Newnham and Paul Guenther at the Province's Housing Policy Branch and Karen Cooper and Laura Kohli at BC Housing.

The graduate seminar is hugely indebted to all the guests who graciously donated their time and expertise to discuss issues candidly with students. And the competition itself owes tremendously to the generous efforts of the jurors who thoughtfully assessed the submissions: Craig Crawford of BC Housing, Liz Evans of the Portland Hotel Society, Bruce Haden of Hotson Bakker Boniface Haden, and Professor George Wagner of the School of Architecture and Landscape Architecture.

Above all, Future Social is the result of the many students who devoted their energy and intelligence to this important topic. To all of them—a big thank you!

CONTENTS

FOREWORD
MATTHEW SOULES

Vancouver is renowned as a model of contemporary urbanism. However, the scope of what constitutes the popular model of Vancouver is narrow. The urbanism, architecture and culture of vast areas of the city are omitted for the sake of the singular clarity of the archetype. One neighbourhood that typically exists outside the bounds of model Vancouver is the Downtown Eastside, a district well-known for its condensed urban poverty and homelessness. The work included in this book is a particular attempt, and an admittedly limited one, to grapple with the issue of housing the homeless of the Downtown Eastside and to add to that work which is positive and already underway. In doing so it asks what the role of architecture is in making the best possible social housing to tackle this problem. In a sense, it aims to glance at a future Vancouver in which its model urbanism folds in the ways that architecture can respond to the issue of homelessness with increasingly superior social housing.

The work in this book is that of students enrolled at the University of British Columbia's School of Architecture and Landscape Architecture. The discussions are between students and guest experts that occurred in a graduate seminar taught in the spring of 2009. The essays are a selection of those produced for the seminar. The design work is the result of an ideas competition for social housing on a specific site in the Downtown Eastside. The competition was open to UBC students and twenty-one entries representing the efforts of over forty students were evaluated by an esteemed jury in the fall of 2009. Included here are the three winners, two honourable mentions, and nine selected non-winning entries.

Taken collectively, it is the hope that the writing and the design propositions shed new light on the topic and the possibilities of social housing for the homeless in Vancouver, in British Columbia, and beyond. Perhaps of equal importance, the work can be seen as a registration of the students' sincere interest in working to produce the best possible cities of the future; cities in which architecture is increasingly responsive to an authentically diverse and varied set of residents.

COMPETITION PARAMETERS

The following is the text describing the architectural ideas competition as it was issued to the entrants.

The Brief

Homelessness is a serious problem throughout the world and Vancouver is no exception. This competition seeks to generate innovative design ideas for supportive housing that meaningfully contribute to solving the problem of homelessness.

At different points in time, societies have created housing for the disadvantaged in a variety of ways. During the mid to late 20th century the federal government of Canada operated national housing programs that included the creation of large scale public housing projects. These projects were developed and operated by the government. For a number of reasons these national programs have been abandoned. At the dawn of the 21st century, the current system for the creation of new non-market housing for the economically disadvantaged foregrounds the role of non-profit organizations that build and operate housing projects. The provincial government administers funding to these non-profit organizations to hire design teams and develop sites in a relatively autonomous manner. This competition asks participants to consider new, future models of design within this contemporary system of housing delivery.

Social housing is a broad umbrella category that includes a spectrum of housing types that can include co-op housing and seniors' housing at one end and emergency shelters at the other. This competition focuses on housing for the homeless and/or those at severe risk of homelessness. Specifically, entrants are asked to design a 'supportive housing' facility. The exact nature of supportive housing is open to participants' creative interpretation but should loosely be understood as housing that incorporates some sort of support services. Typical Vancouver examples of supportive housing usually incorporate a minimum of two support workers, on-site, within the building, at all times to help residents with any needs they may have. The residents of supportive housing often have health problems that frequently include physical disabilities, mental health disorders, and substance abuse/addiction problems. Support may extend to meal services, on-site nurses, counsellors, and doctors, in addition to programs such as job-training, recreation programs, and employment opportunities.

FUTURE SOCIAL challenges you to envision innovative and exciting new types of design for this serious issue.

The Program

This competition calls for designs of a supportive housing facility that caters to formerly homeless people and/or people at a high risk of becoming homeless. The following programmatic requirements must be satisfied:

- » 55 one-person units that:
  - » are self-contained
  - » are secure
  - » include at a minimum: a space to sleep, a space to prepare and eat food, and a bathroom that incorporates a toilet, sink and shower
  - » have exposure to natural light and ventilation
  - » have storage space for personal items
  - » are no larger than 425 ft^2
- » Space for support staff:
  - » The facility will offer, as a minimum, two support workers present 24 hours/day, 7 days/week
- » The facility must be handicap accessible
- » Basic fire egress regulations must be satisfied: At least two exits from each floor area

The above program is a minimum, except for the fact that more units cannot be added. Entrants are encouraged to be creative in its interpretation. Importantly, additional non-unit program can be added as appropriate to a project's conceptual position. For instance: What is the character and disposition of common space? What additional support services can be incorporated into the facility? Does the project include spaces that can be used by the wider community?

The Site

The site is comprised of two adjacent lots, with the following addresses: 5 West Hastings Street and 7 West Hastings Street in the Downtown Eastside neighbourhood of Vancouver. These two lots together form the one site for the competition. Its dimensions are 65'-8" wide and 131'-4" deep.

Both 5 and 7 West Hastings are currently occupied by four-story buildings. For this competition the building at 5 West Hastings will be demolished in its entirety to make way for new construction. Five West Hastings should thus be considered a vacant lot. As is the case with many buildings in the Downtown Eastside, the current building at 7 West Hastings has a heritage bylaw designation. For this competition the Hastings façade must be preserved while the remaining building may be demolished. It is possible to make minor modifications to this façade as appropriate to your project's concept.

It is vital to consider how your design intelligently responds to the façade of 7 West Hastings as well as other aspects of the existing built heritage of the downtown.

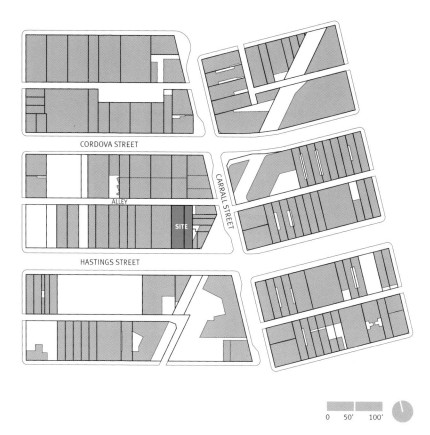

CORDOVA STREET

CARRALL STREET

ALLEY

SITE

HASTINGS STREET

0   50'   100'

Please Note

BC Housing owns 7 West Hastings. The hotel at this address is currently being renovated to meet life safety standards and will be operated by the Portland Hotel Society as a single room occupancy hotel for people who are homeless or at risk of homelessness. The site at 5 West Hastings is in private ownership and there are no government plans to purchase this site at this time. There are no government plans at this time to demolish or redevelop either building. These sites represent a typical example of the kind of development opportunity in the Downtown Eastside but there are no plans to actually develop these sites.

Zoning Considerations

The following are the only zoning issues applicable for this competition:

» Maximum building height: 100'
» Parking: You can elect to incorporate parking into your design but are not required to. Any entry to parking must be from the alley

The Judging Criteria

The jury will give consideration to such characteristics as:

» Originality and innovation
» Enhancement of quality of life for residents
» Cost effectiveness
» Integration of innovative sustainable design strategies and technologies
» Creative response to site and context
» Potential to inform future social housing projects
» Contribution to the community as a whole, beyond the specific site

The Jury

Jury Chair

Matthew Soules, Director, Matthew Soules Architecture and Assistant Professor, School of Architecture and Landscape Architecture, University of British Columbia (non-voting).

Jurors

Craig Crawford, Vice President of Development Services, BC Housing.

Liz Evans, Executive Director, Portland Hotel Society.

Bruce Haden, Principal, Hotson Bakker Boniface Haden.

George Wagner, Professor and Chair of Architecture, School of Architecture and Landscape Architecture, University of British Columbia.

SURVIVAL MODE: *HOME*
MARANATHA COULAS

Homelessness is defined by the United Nations as a condition of either living outdoors, in emergency shelters or hostels, or in housing that does not meet basic UN standards. These standards include adequate protection from the elements, access to safe water and sanitation, affordable prices, and secure tenure and personal safety.[1] Such definitions of homelessness, while useful, tend to emphasize a physical state and undervalue the importance of considering homelessness as a way of life in which particular psychologies develop. Homelessness has been described as: "Being lonely. Scared. Survival."[2] Inherent to the homeless condition are heightened sensitivities to states of marginalization, safety, control, privacy and peace. To be homeless is to be in survival mode. While it is impossible to define a specific psychology of homelessness in which every homeless person fits, an understanding of prevalent psychological phenomena has important implications for social housing that aims to deal with homelessness.

Survival Mode: Marginalization and Homeless Culture

The homeless are perhaps the most marginalized of society. Countless testimonials support this:

> People look at us as subhuman, as almost not people. We're invisible. You ever watch anybody watch a homeless person and they don't see them?[3]

Most people walk straight by, as if you're nothing, as if you don't exist. Some look down their noses at you. Some are really horrible and call you names. Kids are the worst because they come up and kick you when you're lying down.[4]

The marginalization of homeless people has spatial and territorial dimensions. Gabor Maté, a physician working in Vancouver's Downtown Eastside, describes how marginalization results in an invisible barrier which helps confine homeless people to the neighbourhood. "There is a world beyond, but to them it's largely inaccessible. It fears and rejects them and they, in turn, do not understand its rules and cannot survive in it."[5] This polyvalent Other-ing generates a heightened state of loneliness and insecurity.

"Once [homeless], the process of degradation and dehumanization causes a crisis. The need to feel physically, psychologically and emotionally secure, to know that the 'self' and social identity are stable and can remain so, becomes paramount."[6] In order to survive this state of marginalization many of the homeless come together to form what British researcher Megan Ravenhill calls "homeless culture," where the marginalized can effectively become "mainstream" within their own community, accepted for who they are and provided with an alternative means to ontological security.[7] "Once there they become part of a continuum of social exclusion and inclusion where people on the margins of mainstream society move into and through the homeless culture (bobbing in and out)—a culture that developed or evolved around the support needs of this group. It caters for people's need to belong, to be respected."[8] Homeless culture plays an important role in serving the needs of the homeless which cannot be met or understood within mainstream society and to some extent empowers its members.[9]

Ravenhill further describes homeless culture as constituted by dense social networks, reciprocity, and friendship. Care is demonstrated amongst its members. The marginalization that the homeless experience and the social acceptance which is offered by homeless culture create an affinity between its members as well as to the spaces in which the homeless culture is embedded. "The intense friendship and reciprocal care received within the homeless culture seems not to be prevalent in mainstream society. The lack of an alternative within housed society may contribute to the marginalization of people dependent on or in need of such care, effectively forcing people to remain within the homeless culture."[10]

The importance of homeless culture is evidenced in the difficulties that formerly homeless people commonly experience once housed. Many experience, not only culture shock, but separation anxiety and depression upon being extracted from their support networks and systems of ontological security.[11] "Evidence suggests that these support systems made leaving the streets difficult as the vulnerable often had to leave the people they had relied on for their life, sanity and survival. It was hard to let go of that level of support, knowing that there was no equivalent for them in mainstream society."[12]

In her book, *The Healing House*, Barbara Bannon Harwood states: "It is important to understand that our homes are truly extensions of ourselves in perhaps an even more profound way than we realize when we say that people buy homes to fit their needs. We buy our image of what we 'belong' in."[13] Anti-poverty activist Sheila Baxter further states: "Home is associated with personal identity, family, relationships, a role in the community, privacy and security, and the possession of personal property. Homelessness or the lack of a home affects all these areas of an individual's life."[14]

If homes are an extension of ourselves and where we belong, as these authors suggest, it might be logical to suggest that social housing for the homeless should in some way manifest the spaces in which homeless culture is embedded. To further this point Maté refers to the street in relation to one man's life as, "[t]he only home he's ever had—a phrase that sums up the histories of many people in Vancouver's Downtown Eastside."[15] The street is the familiar territory where homeless culture exists. In order for social housing to most effectively house the homeless it would perhaps be beneficial to translate street spaces and their social elements into housing.[16]

What might this look like? Sou Fujimoto's, House N in Oita, Japan, while a private single family home, presents an interesting example of this possibility. The house consists of three volumes of decreasing size, one inside another. The outer shell fills the site and creates a covered, semi-indoor garden. The second shell, inside the first, encloses space inside the covered outdoor space, while the third shell, inside the second, creates yet a smaller interior and more private space.[17] Fujimoto states:

> I have always had doubts about streets and houses being separated by a single wall, and wondered that a gradation of rich domain accompanied by various senses of distance between streets and houses might be a possibility, such as: a place inside the house that is fairly near the street; a place that is a bit far from the street, and a place far off the street, in secure privacy. That is why life in this house resembles to living among the clouds. A distinct boundary is nowhere to be found, except for a gradual change in the domain. One might say that an ideal architecture is an outdoor space that feels like the indoors and an indoor space that feels like the outdoors. In a nested structure, the inside is invariably the outside, and vice versa. My intention was to make an architecture that is not about space nor about form, but simply about expressing the riches of what are 'between' houses and streets.[18]

This idea of 'between' space, one which smoothes the boundaries between the indoors and outdoors, or street and home, creates an opportunity for the translation of homeless cultural space to the space of social housing for the homeless. It provides a glimpse of possibility for a gradated social space between the outdoor street and the inner private domain. Talmadge Wright, in his analysis of homeless geographies, discusses the relationship between placemaking and identity in relation to shared social space:

> Creating 'safe' spaces in which to gather is essential [...]. It is not as if we have homeless placemaking, and that leads to collective identities. Homeless placemaking is one side of the development of collective

House N, Sou Fujimoto, Oita, Japan, 2007. Photographs by Iwan Baan.

identity, and collective identity is the other side of homeless placemaking. Understanding integration of placemaking and collective identity leads to understanding the importance of the formation of collective places, spaces given a particular social meaning by a group.[19]

The provision of shared social spaces which can translate homeless culture into social housing, embracing the riches of what lies between housing and the streets, may be a way to reinforce and augment the positive aspects of the support networks and self-identities that the homeless establish for survival.

Survival Mode: Safety

Heightened concern for personal security and safety is also intrinsic to being in survival mode. For many homeless, the feeling of safety is not a part of their everyday experience, but rather the contrary. They experience violence and fear for personal safety on a regular basis. Wright describes how, "the one factor that seemed consistent for all the squatters was the *desire for safety* [and] [t]he shelters were believed to be unsafe places where one could not be protected from predatory elements."[20] Often the homeless have to rely on each other for their personal safety. One woman quoted in *Homeless: True stories of life on the streets*, states:

> The hardest part of it all was if I had to be sleeping out anywhere by myself. Even if I was on the street I'd at least have one male with me for safety. I'm a big girl and I can handle myself, but there's no way I'd put myself in that situation again. Bad things do happen. Some [female] friends of mine suffered worse; they ended up stuffed into sports bags and dumped in the river.[21]

For those who have experienced homelessness, sensitivity to personal safety levels is heightened. Security in social housing for the homeless should thus be made tangible to its residents.

Adolf Loos's Rufer and Muller houses provide a provocative example of ways in which security can become legible. In both instances Loos separates physical and visual connections between spaces. In both houses a visual connection between the dining room and adjacent music room is made via a wide opening, yet the dining room is raised from the music room in a manner that does not allow any direct physical movement between the two spaces. Beatriz Colomina, the architectural historian, refers to this strategy of physical separation combined with visual connection as an act of 'framing' everyday domestic life.[22] The visual framing of space in this manner can be equated to establishing the ability to safely observe the related spaces of one's surroundings from a space which feels secure.

The act of establishing a legible sense of safety through visual access combined with physical separation can take place through a wide diversity of architectural techniques. While Loos pursues a spatial strategy, another example is architect Wiel Arets' use of materials to achieve a comparable effect in his social housing project in Tilburg, Holland. Throughout the project there is an extensive use of glass blocks, not only in the exterior envelope but also within the interior as a means of physically separating spaces. Circulation and shared social spaces are enclosed with glass block. Spaces are physically separated yet any presence or movement can still be detected and observed from a safe vantage point.

Visually connecting spaces while physically separating them allows for a level of awareness of that engenders a heightened sense of safety that is of increased importance for those transitioning from homelessness.

Survival Mode: Control

"I don't like the term homeless[...] [b]ecause it's more than not having a home. It should be powerlessness. Because you just lose every human right you can imagine when you're homeless."[23] The homeless condition of being in survival mode often results in heightened sensitivities to states of control and space plays an important role.

Ravenhill describes space being appropriated by the homeless in order to gain a sense of control:

> The occupation and ownership of space was a powerful part of identity, self-preservation and to a certain extent self-worth. Space was strongly connected with power. It gave the roofless the power to make people walk a different route, to walk round them, to see them, to see their rooflessness, to see what rooflessness had done to their bodies, their clothes. Space gave the roofless the power to alienate, repulse and intimidate passers-by. [...] Simply occupying doorways or a set of park benches created no-go areas.[24]

While surveillance in social housing is usually used as a tool to monitor residents and guests, it can also be a device that offers residents a sense of control through their own occupation of space. Since social housing usually consists of a series of private individual units that are connected with some kind of shared circulation space, it is possible to reconsider the relationship between the occupation of private space in relation to semi-public spaces in terms of control on the part of residents.

Loos's residential interiors are once again helpful in thinking how this can occur. In the Muller house, as Colomina explains, a sense of control is "not achieved by simply turning one's back on the exterior and immersing oneself in a private universe. [...] It is no longer the house that is a theater box; there is a theater box inside the house, overlooking the internal social spaces [...] The classical distinction between inside and outside, private and public, object and subject, becomes convoluted."[25] The 'theatre box' conception of spatial organization enables domestic voyeurism and forms of control. Colomina further elucidates:

> [T]he most intimate room is like a theater box, placed just over the entrance to the social spaces in this house, so that any intruder could easily be seen. Likewise, the view of the exterior, towards the city, from

this 'theater box,' is contained within a view of the interior. Suspended in the middle of the house, this space assumes both the character of a 'sacred' space and of a point of control. Comfort is paradoxically produced by two seemingly opposing conditions, intimacy and control.[26]

This coupling of comfort and control, while perhaps fundamental to all domestic conditions, is key to making successful spaces to house the homeless.

Loos's specific positioning of more private space in visual relation to more social space, creates a sense of control simply through occupation of that private space. As Colomina suggests, "architecture is not simply a platform that accommodates the viewing subject. It is a viewing mechanism that produces the subject. It precedes and frames its occupant."[27] The position and disposition of private space can play a role in social housing for the homeless to address an individual's sense of control and its very nature can also be specific to the psychologies of homelessness.

Survival Mode: Privacy

While Ravenhill observes that the homeless often use space as a means of asserting forms of control she also notes:

Space was [...] used for retreat, to hide or to become anonymous. By finding a space away from public view (a rooftop, an underground car park or a graveyard) people retreated to their space and stored or hid possessions, creating a sense of safety [...]. Space, therefore, was simultaneously a means of identity and anonymity, a way of standing out or disappearing and a means of power for the comparatively powerless.[28]

Inherent to the homeless condition of being in survival mode is a heightened sensitivity to privacy.

The United Nations Centre for Human Settlements describes homeless people as "the pavement dwellers, those who must sleep in doorways, subways, and recesses of public buildings[...]."[29] The prospects of actually being able to effectively sleep is a vital and fundamental concern for homeless people that is connected to both safety and privacy. According to Ravenhill, "[l]ocation is key, especially for people sleeping on their own. Some locations increase safety, for example a loading bay – raised off the ground, walls to three sides, a roof, out of the way of pedestrians."[30] This suggests that the experience of sleeping in public spaces may create a relationship to a specific type of space in which one is able to sleep. Such spatialized sleeping habits can continue once an individual is housed. The widespread practice of sleeping in doorways, in areas raised off the ground, or in a space with walls to three sides suggests that a different type of spatial treatment for sleeping spaces in social housing for the formerly homeless may be appropriate in some instances.

It may be advantageous to provide sleeping spaces that translate the form of spatial privacy and safety that was comforting on the streets. An example is the sleeping space in the Swedish architecture firm Bunker Hill's housing project in Stockholm that is raised nearly to the ceiling and enclosed on three sides. While the strategy is used in this case to save space, it can also be employed in social housing for the homeless to provide highly protected and private sleeping space for those who are accustomed to and only able to sleep under specific spatial circumstances.

Survival Mode: Peace

Yale sociologist Michael Rowe discusses the existence of a 'crazy-making' aspect of homelessness, which he describes as "a dual effect of concrete physical deficits such as hunger and lack of sleep, and the cumulative toll of anxiety, lack of normal social contact, and loss of self-esteem."[31] Countless testimonials of homeless people verify the prevalence of constant anxiety, worry, and irritability. It is important that social housing for the homeless consider the ways in which it can respond to this psychological condition. One of the possible methods can be architecture's positioning of 'nature.'

Wright investigated the experiences of those living in a squatter settlement known as "Tranquility City" in Chicago. The site included tall bushes, trees, and wildlife. One squatter described it as "the most beautiful

11 Square Meters, Bunker Hill, Stockholm, Sweden, 2006. Photograph courtesy of Bunker Hill.

place."[32] He said, "It was peaceful. We had every type of animal there."[33] In considering the thoughts of Tranquility residents, Wright concluded that the natural peacefulness of the site offered a "location where they could think and repair their lives [that] contrasted not only with the world of shelters but also with the world of public housing projects."[34] The anxiety experienced during homelessness can often continue when a person becomes housed. Culture shock, new responsibilities, and noisy residents can all contribute to the continued experience of anxiety. The survival mode phenomenon of peace seeking in natural environments suggests that aspects of the natural environment might be effectively applied in social housing.

Water features can be effective not only in producing white noise to mask disturbing sounds, they can also generate calming effects. Bannon describes how "[w]hen one relaxes with those memories [of natural sounds], medical studies show, heart rate and blood pressure drop, beneficial hormones are produced in the brain—which triggers the immune system to function more effectively—and alpha brainwaves begin to tune up, increasing creativity."[35]

Additionally, plants can produce peaceful psychological effects. Christopher Day, in his analysis of the architecture of healing, states:

> Green is a colour of balance; it has a peaceful, calming, soothing effect. Yet it requires considerable skill to paint a room in opaque green without it becoming heavy and dead, for green is such a lifeless colour to paint with. Worse than that, there's the risk that reflected light will green people's face creating, by association, a disquieting mood. By contrast, light shining in through foliage can be both life-filled and peace bringing.[36]

It is exciting to consider the ways in which plant-life can be integrated into social housing for the homeless in innovative ways that can enhance peacefulness.

Alternative to the use of living natural elements, the production of nature-like phenomena may evoke similar feelings to those experienced in an authentic natural environment. For example, Tattoo House in Victoria, Australia, by Andrew Maynard Architects, applies a super-graphic 'tattoo' pattern of trees on its exterior glazing as a way to filter light and views in and out of the interior. The dappled interior light recreates an effect similar to being within a natural treed setting.

The provision of peaceful architectural settings is of increased importance for those who are transitioning from homelessness to social housing and the deployment of both natural and artificial 'natures' is one particularly rich strategy.

Conclusion

Those without a safe and secure home may show "behaviors from which psychopathology is inferred [but which] might be better understood as behavioral adaptations to the trying exigencies of street life rather than as symptomatic psychiatric impairment." [...] The experience of homelessness "includes the psychosocial pain associated with constant denigration, humiliation, neglect, [...] social and economic isolation, [...] post-trauma physical illness, supranormal experiences, food and sleep disorders, disorientation, phobias, victimization by particular individuals/systems/states, and recidivism."[37]

The challenges that the homeless face are many, and the more these challenges are understood, less as strictly the physical state of homelessness, but more as a comprehensive way of life from which particular psychologies are developed, the better they may be housed. By considering only some of the heightened sensitivities that the homeless experience in survival mode it is evident how social housing can be better designed to house the homeless.

1. Lyne Casavant, "Definition of Homelessness" in *Homelessness* (Ottawa: Government of Canada, 1999), accessed August 4, 2011, http://dsp-psd.pwgsc.gc.ca/Collection-R/LoPBdP/modules/prb99-1-homelessness/definition-e.htm#DEFINITIONtxt.

2. Tom C. Allen, *Someone To Talk To: Care and Control of the Homeless* (Halifax: Fernwood Publishing, 2000), 77.

3. Homeless person quoted in Michael Rowe, *Crossing the Border: Encounters Between Homeless People and Outreach Workers* (Berkeley: University of California Press, 1999), 44.

4. Tommy, male, aged 35, homeless, quoted in Megan Ravenhill, *The Culture of Homelessness* (Cornwall: Ashgate Publishing, 2008), 157.

5. Gabor Maté, *In the Realm of Hungry Ghosts: Close Encounters with Addiction* (Toronto: Alfred A. Knopf, 2008), 20.

6. Ravenhill, *The Culture of Homelessness*, 158.

7. Ibid, 157.

8. Ibid, 145.

9. Ibid, 145.

10. Ibid, 155.

11. Ibid, 146.

12. Ibid, 163.

13. Barbara Bannon Harwood, *The Healing House: How Living in the Right House Can Heal You Spiritually, Emotionally, and Physically* (Carlsbad: Hay House, 1997), 1.

14. Sheila Baxter, *Under the Viaduct: Homeless in Beautiful B.C.* (Vancouver: New Star Books, 1991), 8.

15. Maté, *In the Realm of Hungry Ghosts*, 13.

16. Ibid, 13.

17. Sou Fujimoto, "House N," *GA Houses 98* (2007): 74.

18. Ibid, 74.

19. Talmadge Wright, *Out of Place: Homeless Mobilizations, Subcities, and Contested Landscapes* (Albany: State University of New York Press, 1997), 262.

20. Ibid, 281.

21. Andrew Byrne, *Homeless: True stories of life on the streets* (Sydney: New Holland Publishers, 2005), 34.

22. Beatriz Colomina, "The split wall: domestic voyeurism," in *Housing and Dwelling: Perspectives on Modern Domestic Architecture*, ed. Barbara Miller Lane (New York: Routledge, 2007), 85.

23. Rowe, *Crossing the Border*, 44.

24. Ravenhill, *The Culture of Homelessness*, 178.

25. Colomina, "The split wall," 83.

26. Ibid, 83.

27. Ibid, 84.

28. Ravenhill, *The Culture of Homelessness*, 179.

29. Baxter, *Under the Viaduct*, 10.

30. Ravenhill, *The Culture of Homelessness*, 177.

31. Rowe, *Crossing the Border*, 30.

32. Wright, *Out of Place*, 279.

33. Ibid, 279.

34. Ibid, 280.

35. Harwood, *The Healing House*, 109.

36. Christopher Day, *Places of the Soul: Architecture and Environmental Design as a Healing Art* (Burlington: Architectural Press, 2004), 73.

37. Quotation of Snow et al (1986): 421 and Barak (1990):8 in Allen, *Someone To Talk To*, 22.

THE POLITICS OF SOCIAL HOUSING
JANUARY 12, 2009

A discussion between graduate students and guests.

GUESTS

Craig Crawford, Vice President of Development Services, BC Housing.

Jim O'Dea, Terra Housing Consultants.

Stuart Thomas, Terra Housing Consultants.

STUDENTS

Magali Bailey, Rebecca Bateman, Bryan Beça, Maranatha Coulas, Stephanie da Silva, Idette de Boer, Anya Georgivejic, Andrea Hoff, Meghan McBride, Rodrigo Ferrari Nunes and Matt Purvis.

PROFESSOR

Matthew Soules

DISCUSSION

....

de Boer	**I am curious to learn more about the current financing mechanisms for social housing in British Columbia.**
Crawford	During construction, BC Housing finances any given building with interim construction financing. BC Housing has access to funds that it can loan at a reasonably low interest rate (now at 1.3%). The Canadian Mortgage and Housing Corporation (CMHC)

insure mortgages that non-profit housing societies enter into. Near the end of the construction phase we'll tender out these long term mortgages. The banks know that they're insured by CMHC and that BC Housing will be flowing subsidies. Since they are low risk, non-profit societies get low interest rates. A society will sign a 35-year mortgage and then they start operation. The overflow of the mortgage subsidy is paid back over the 35 year term.

de Boer   **What kind of guarantee is there for the CMHC that the subsidy will be repaid?**

Crawford   We sign an operating agreement with the non-profit housing society which commits us to owing that mortgage for 35 years. Plus we have an agreement with the CMHC that we won't allow the mortgage to go into default. If a particular society disappears then we'll find another non-profit society to take over. This approach allows the societies to lead the development, get mortgages, and operate the buildings—not the government. This is different than in the 1950s and 1960s when government directly ran the programs. We now have a more community based model of housing development.

de Boer   **With the subsidies, how does BC Housing know they will have access to funding from the province for 35 years?**

Crawford   Government understands the funding model and supports it.

Hoff   **Is cost the reason you do not want different types of units? Socially speaking, it could be a great advantage to have a very diverse mix of units in a project.**

Crawford   It depends. In downtown Vancouver we could have a mix of two, three and even four bedroom units. In the current context of what we're doing with the 12 and 14 sites in Vancouver that are specifically for the homeless population there is a distinct population we work with. Beyond having a self-contained bachelor unit of around 325 ft^2, which could in the future house a senior, an individual with an illness or a student, we don't see the value of having a mix of units.

Coulas	**Could you describe BC Housing's design guidelines and construction standards?**
Crawford	We have a mix of performance and prescriptive guidelines that we use private consultants to give us direction on. We also get feedback on durability from users, non-profit societies and our own property portfolio managers. The focus on envelope design has shifted to the current theme of energy and sustainability.
da Silva	**The C-Side building in Vancouver's Coal Harbour has shared elevators for both market renters and social housing tenants while the Woodward's development in the Downtown Eastside has separate elevators. Is there a simple way to make that decision, and do you think one is more successful than the other?**
Crawford	The Affordable Housing Society is the non-profit society involved in both C-Side and the Woodward's building.
O'Dea	The Affordable Housing Society was leasing the site for C-Side from the City and they were responsible for the whole design. At Woodward's, the developer drove the design of the project and Affordable Housing was only responsible for their specific social housing units so they didn't have a say about the entrance design. There is a different mentality when developing a project where there is home ownership in place. Home owners generally don't like rental units regardless of whether they're social housing or not. Owners can try to control the number of renters through by-laws, whereas in rental projects the mixing is different.
Thomas	At the C-Side, the plan was originally to have separate elevators but it was logistically impossible. Affordable Housing and the City were anxious about the entrance and elevator situation, but when the project was built the shared elevators were never an issue.
Nunes	**In your opinion, what is the best way to handle the NIMBY phenomena?**
Crawford	For the 12 Vancouver sites for social housing that are currently in development, we signed a Memorandum of Understanding that identified the sites and each was presented to city council. The City planned a series of public meetings before going to

council in which we specifically talked about how these projects would be housing the homeless and drug addicts. In the council meetings, people consistently stood up saying: "This is great but we need more of it." Since there isn't much social housing on the West Side of Vancouver, there was concern about the Dunbar location. However, the City of Vancouver had explained their plan to provide affordable housing throughout the city before the three-day public meeting process started. The City's plan is that every neighbourhood gets its share so that services are not concentrated in one area. This plan seemed to pave the way for a broader acceptance throughout the city.

It is important for residents to know that these projects are safe and what they can do if there's a problem. People often think that having social housing nearby will decrease their property value, but that's not true.

Beça	**I'm curious about the issue of tenureship. Are there other methods that might be put into practice like co-ops or long term leaseholds?**
O'Dea	Not really. The big thing is trying to get affordable rentals built because there's already lots of home ownership. On one project we tried group ownership where each person owned a share that was a freehold title. It has worked, but it's hard to manage when someone wants to leave.
Beça	In Europe they have long term lease holdings where you don't own the property but you have a lease for a long time.
O'Dea	There are even 999 year leases. Technically in terms of financing, the lender would fund you 100% of your purchase but they use the lease to control your design. This happens in subdivisions so you can't change anything without the approval of a body. It has no effect on value. In BC, a 60 year lease is worth about 75% of freehold value.
Coulas	**Coal Harbour is among the most expensive real estate in Vancouver. Why is there social housing there?**

O'Dea   Selective and elitist communities like Shaughnessy are just as bad as the Downtown Eastside. However, we can only provide balanced communities for low- and middle-income groups. Higher income communities can afford their own architects to create by-laws, and get them passed by city council, creating their own system. Mixed neighbourhoods, like Coal Harbour are more desirable. When developers buy land and get it rezoned, significantly increasing the value of their land, the City is giving them a lot. The developer should have to give something back to the community like nice open areas, walkways, daycares and affordable housing.

Crawford   Walkways and open spaces are public goods but affordable housing is a private good, so that's a problematic comparison. You can have a dilemma like what occurs in Whistler where the employees need affordable housing. From a community based perspective it makes a lot of sense to have mixed income communities. The fairness and allocation is a question that is hard to answer.

O'Dea   Only the City can make these things happen through zoning. They can require a permit process to put in a walkway but they need special zoning for social housing.

               Poor do benefit by being around the rich, not because they have access to better people, but because they have access to better services.

Crawford   Social housing can act as a vehicle for improving a depressed neighbourhood. When more people come into a neighbourhood better services are demanded.

Soules   **One of the issues concerning the design of social housing seems to be its relation to what we might call exceptional design. Outstanding design is often perceived as a waste of tax dollars. This is a condition that generally doesn't exist in the private sector. This mentality may reinforce mediocrity and could be seen as a disincentive for advancement of all sorts. How do we deal with that as designers, policy makers, and thinkers? The projects for the 14 sites are providing**

29

leadership in terms of sustainability. How is it possible to take a leadership role for future projects by demonstrating that great design doesn't necessarily need to be expensive?

Crawford   When the architecture is celebrated, it increases the dignity of the residents and raises the profile of social housing. When a project is successful, some people think that architects spent too much to make monuments to themselves. We don't want architects to forget our goals just to win awards. On LEED we are proud to be in the forefront. We are using LEED as an educational vehicle, and we have passed on information to the private sector who in turn can implement similar strategies. The whole of society will benefit. On the design side, it's just human nature.

Bateman   Regarding NIMBYism and trying to counteract it, it appears to often lead to buildings that fit in but become anonymous. If it doesn't blend in, people wonder why so much is being spent on these people. It goes back to societal attitudes about the deserving and undeserving poor.

O'Dea   Attractive buildings have value but they don't have to stand out, just look good. It contributes to community acceptance.

Crawford   We should also be aware that construction costs, while important, pale in comparison to the cost of support services. We have to consider the relative costs versus the operating costs.

Soules   We're talking about the place of good architecture in social housing. I'm concerned about the way in which ideology and power put a set of constraints on social housing that don't exist elsewhere in the housing continuum. The government has been a leader in sustainability, but how can we also raise the design standards of the built environment as a whole?

Crawford   BC Housing's impact on design should be small as we are program administrators. We want architects to do their best with the budget.

O'Dea   When non-profits interview architects, they want to know if they design from the inside or from the outside. The non-profits are concerned with the inside. They want considerate and appropriate designs for the tenants. It is therefore important to have the non-profits involved from the start.

Crawford   One of the unintentional consequences of the LEED process is that it has all disciplines collaborating from the beginning of a project which is very helpful.

Soules   **What's the interface between BC Housing and other government agencies, such as the Ministry of Health, given that the 14 sites are all for supportive housing?**

Crawford   When two completely different government agencies get together, timing and processes for getting budgets become complicated. As we moved into the homeless portfolio, BC Housing started getting capital for housing and the Health Ministry started getting funds for support. It was difficult to coordinate. Now BC Housing also requests funding for support services. Levels of support vary and the Health Ministry helps us to support the hardest-to-house.

Coulas   **At what point are the residents who are going to live in these projects brought into the process?**

O'Dea   There is no general rule; different non-profits do it in different ways. With supportive housing we don't know exactly who will be moving in so there is more involvement with property management and staff.

Soules   **How is a design team usually chosen?**

Crawford   BC Housing will usually get some funding and have a proposal call. We want the non-profits to come as a team with a chosen site, a builder, and an architect. Very rarely do we directly hire architects or builders.

Soules   So BC Housing usually evaluates a series of proposals?

Crawford   Yes. At one point we asked for a schematic design and a fixed price from a developer but it drove up the cost of submission and inexperienced groups were excluded. Over the years we have lowered the bar. We just want a well organized group that knows what they're doing so they can run the building for the next 60 years.

Thomas   But people still need to prepare more information than required to get any serious consideration. You basically need an architect to create a schematic design in order to choose a site. Back to the question about getting residents involved in the design

	process, it seems like you were implying they don't get a chance to participate because it is social housing. Buyers don't usually get to participate in the design of market dwellings either. We often use expert front line people or focus groups to ensure the interests of users.
Crawford	We have a ten-year history without design rules but have managed to reach a commonality in unit design by working with non-profits, user groups, and tenants.
de Boer	**How often does Vancouver's "20% rule" for social housing actually happen?**
Crawford	Unfortunately, it is somewhat historical. It was based on the assumption that the provincial and federal governments would provide the developers with money to fulfill that 20% requirement for social housing. It was more for the redevelopment of sites, not specific density bonuses related to specific buildings.
Bateman	When tenants are brought into the design we find that the focus groups want very basic things, especially if they have been living in SROs. It reveals their priorities, indicating that some things may not be universal.
Crawford	BC Housing and architects build many projects, whereas a single non-profit typically builds only a few. It's important that each respects the expertise of the other.
Coulas	I think that social housing differs from market housing since market buyers have greater choice.
O'Dea	Non-profits have different management styles and tenants are drawn to different ones.
Thomas	Different non-profits also have different histories.
O'Dea	They have different designs too. Homeless people are not a homogenous group.

WINNING ENTRIES

This winning scheme satisfies multiple criteria with a clever simplicity and refined generosity.

A two-level plinth incorporates community services such as employment counselling and a bicycle repair shop. Atop this plinth the 55 units and their associated shared spaces form an 'S' shape in plan; thereby shaping two courtyards for building tenants. The roof-scape of this 'S' steps up from the Hastings Street heritage façade in a series of rooftop garden terraces. This overall building form carefully responds to the site's context while providing abundant natural light and air in a manner that gently encourages dynamic community interaction within the building.

At the scale of the unit, the typical narrow plan has been replaced by the square. The washroom, cooking appliances, and storage are all condensed along two walls, thereby liberating the majority of the space for open-plan living. One exterior-facing wall has folding doors that can open up entirely to the balcony. The result is a refreshing perceptual spaciousness in small-unit living. Residents are free to modestly customize their units by constructing simple partitions in the building's mill-work shop and installing them as desired.

SELF-SUSTAINING BUILDING

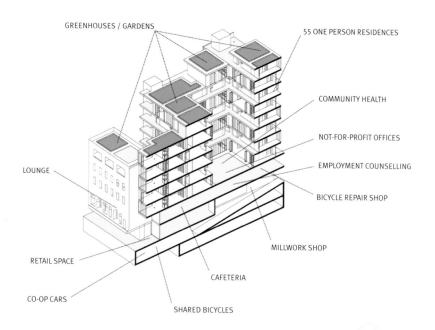

GREENHOUSES / GARDENS

55 ONE PERSON RESIDENCES

COMMUNITY HEALTH

NOT-FOR-PROFIT OFFICES

EMPLOYMENT COUNSELLING

LOUNGE

BICYCLE REPAIR SHOP

MILLWORK SHOP

RETAIL SPACE

CO-OP CARS

CAFETERIA

SHARED BICYCLES

FORM DEVELOPMENT

1. REPEAT UNIT

2. PROVIDE LIGHT & AIR

3. RAISE ABOVE THE STREET

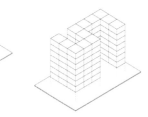

4. SHAPE FOR VIEW, LIGHT & DENSITY

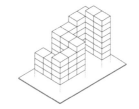

7 WEST HASTINGS

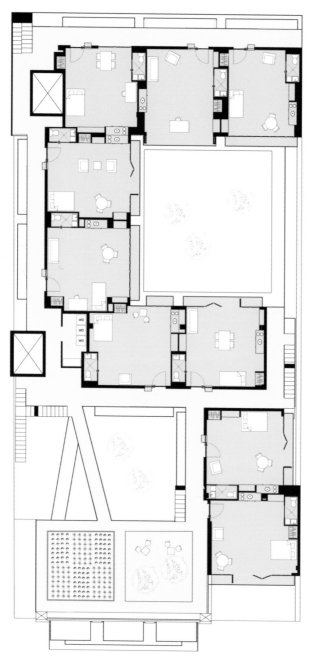

7TH FLOOR

FUTURE SOCIAL

UNIT SECTIONS

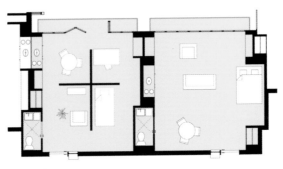

UNIT PLANS

SECOND PRIZE
THE DOROTHY HOUSE
DANIEL IRVINE
ELIZABETH LAING
ARIEL MIELING

Dorothy House focuses its design on the needs of mothers who are in the process of regaining or have recently regained custody of their children from the Ministry of Children and Family Development. In responding to the needs of this user group, the scheme divides the building's living units into a series of sub-communities of eight units that are each organized around a double-height shared space. This shared space includes kitchen, dining, and television areas and is intended to function, in part, as a location in which support staff work with tenants to enhance mothering skills.

The ground floor is devoted to building-wide shared space and community-oriented functions while the units rise above in two separate towers that enclose a courtyard between them.

Each unit is separated from the neighbouring unit by a thickened wall that absorbs a variety of functions. The wall offers storage space and a dining alcove while incorporating bunk-bed like sleeping nooks for children. In this manner, the design demonstrates how relatively simple elements can offer a high-degree of value for particular tenants; in this case, children.

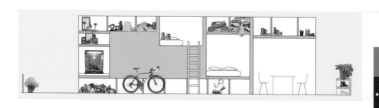

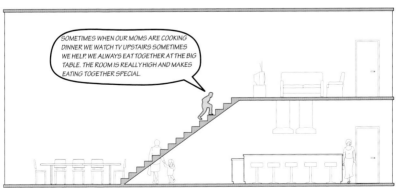

COMMON LIVING AREA SECTION

GROUND FLOOR

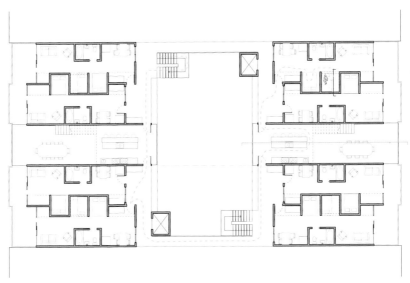

TYPICAL UPPER FLOOR

45

Triune incorporates a range of support services along with different unit types in a finely tuned gradient of movement and use.

A semi-public courtyard behind the heritage façade acts as a filter-like gathering space for the larger community and the building. Beyond the courtyard, the lobby and its reception oversees entry and exit. A large stair connects this space to a communal dining area on the second floor. A modest 24-hour combined medical and mental health clinic sits on the third floor and directly underneath the resident's private courtyard. The stair that connects the clinic and the courtyard allows the clinic's light to act as a glowing beacon of support to the units that overlook the space.

On the third floor the units wrap around the medical clinic while on the upper floors the units are arranged into an 'L' plan that frames the courtyard. To accommodate a range of tenants there are three unit types: Small secure units in close proximity to the clinic, larger single units for more self-sufficient living, and a two-level unit designed for cohabitation with a partner.

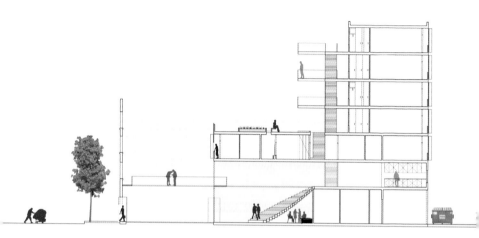

NORTH/SOUTH SECTION

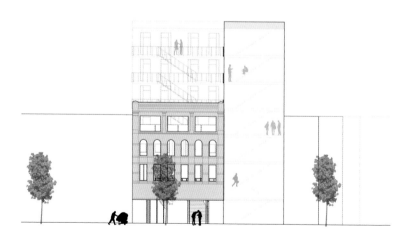

HASTINGS STREET ELEVATION

3RD FLOOR

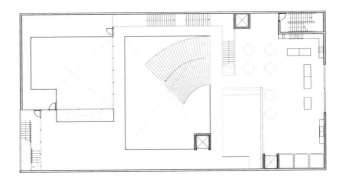

2ND FLOOR

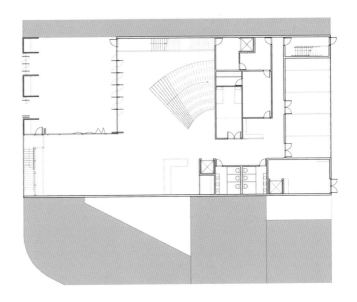

GROUND FLOOR

49

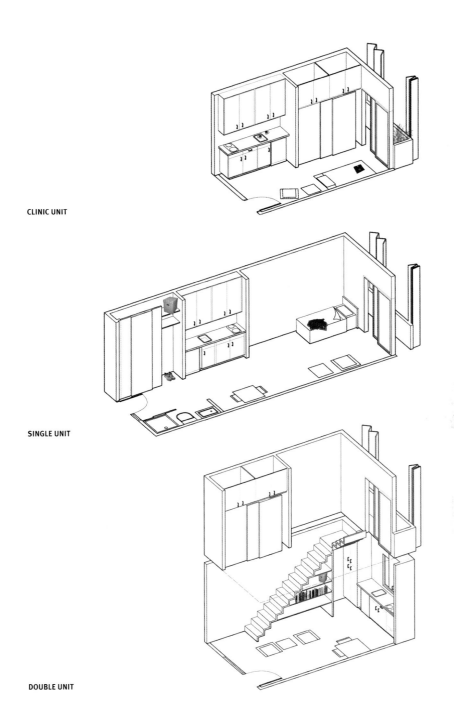

CLINIC UNIT

SINGLE UNIT

DOUBLE UNIT

SMALL MOVES
ARCHITECTURAL STRATEGIES FOR THE UNIT IN SOCIAL HOUSING
ANDREA HOFF

In a framework tending towards the standard, housing continues to constitute a highly sclerotic field characterised by conventionalism and repetition of archetypes.[1] —The Metapolis Dictionary of Advanced Architecture

Architecture—be it at macro or micro level—must not only be a showpiece of design and technology, but also give expression to those democratic ideals of respect for human dignity, equality and freedom that are fostered in our society.[2] —Ralph Erskine

Contemporary North American social housing typically incorporates residential units that are substantially smaller than those in market housing. This limitation of area, and by extension volume, is of course due to the budgetary constraints that surround the production of social housing. This necessary smallness is often perceived as a shortcoming—but it isn't an inherent weakness if the unit is designed appropriately. However, the design of typical social housing fails to deploy strategies that respond to the unique particularities of the small unit. While the status quo approach is, more or less, to shrink a typical market unit to an 'appropriate' size without any other significant recalibration, this paper considers strategies that offer a more fundamental response in which design operates in specific ways to make the most of a small unit. The paper focuses on three such strategies: hyper efficiency, spatial complexity and cross programming. Examples that sometimes lie outside the realm of social housing are drawn upon in an effort to expand design possibilities. While these strategies are not only applicable to social housing, they are here thought of in relation to social housing with the belief that when considered collectively they can offer an array of benefits for those most in need.

Hyper Efficiency

> The homes I like best are completely occupied, busy, and useful. I find smaller spaces—comfy spaces—better than great big houses that are hardly used. By comfy I mean full of books and things that people are doing.[3] —Martha Stewart

Hyper efficiency is a strategy that seeks to maximize the use and functionality of space inside the unit. In a hyper efficient unit, no space is unused or under-used; all possible space has dual, triple, or even quadruple purposes. For example, a hyper efficient wall does not simply function only as a wall but also as a storage or display unit. The operative design pre-occupation becomes determining what important functions can be packed into elements like a floor-plate, window sill, table, and the space adjacent to a refrigerator.

While the list of possible functions to double or triple purpose is extensive, storage is particularly important in social housing. Despite common perception, the majority of tenants, including the previously homeless, have significant personal belongings. This reality is at odds with the size constraints on social housing that place a premium on storage space. There is a clear need for more convenient storage within the social housing unit which hyper efficiency can help address.

Passenger vehicles such as trains, buses, and airplanes are designed for high intensity use within the confines of small spaces and offer compelling precedents for hyper efficient social housing units. As an example, Aranguren & Gallegos' social housing in Carabanchel, Spain draws upon luggage storage within train compartments as a model for new unit efficiencies. Here, furniture such as beds and a table can slide away under the floor of the raised circulation hall, thereby freeing up space for other uses. As Aranguren and Gallegos state:

> We believe that our design proposal of raised corridors and mobile walls is not at all outrageous, and even perhaps excessively possibilistic: for practically the same cost the dwelling gains a greater degree of potential uses by being able to use the majority of the house area as a single space for multiple activities like work, leisure, games, gymnastics, parties, etc. [...] We must reinvent the domestic space, make small spaces large, and make transformable space by means of furniture and features.[4]

Hyper efficiency can be a method that meets the unique requirements of residents while overcoming the spatial limitations so often present in social housing.

Spatial Complexity

> High-quality design encompasses an array of considerations, such as proportion, sense of identity, size and rhythms of openings, circulation, access to light and air, sense of place, and the creation of spaces that are safe, easy to maintain, and suitable for the activities that take place in them. If a development does not address these considerations effectively, it is not well designed, no matter how large it is or how many expensive finishes, fixtures, and appliances it contains.[5]
> —Kathleen Dorgan and Deane Evans

Carabanchel Housing, Aranguren & Gallegos, Madrid, Spain, 2003. Photographs by Hisao Suzuki.

Final Wooden House, Sou Fujimoto, Kumamoto, Japan, 2005. Photograph by Iwan Baan.

Spatial complexity is a strategy to generate the perception that a small space is larger than in it is. It achieves this through the radical diversification of the interior itself and also of the interior and its relation to its exterior. Spatial complexity posits that a spatially diverse interior feels larger than a spatially homogenous interior. It is a configuration of space that goes beyond a singular and cohesive set of four walls, a floor, and a ceiling. While considering functionality it seeks opportunities to shift floor, ceiling, and wall planes into diverse and varied conditions.

Different zones within an interior can be established by changes in ceiling and floor height. Through such techniques a space can simultaneously be perceptually one, two, or more. This differentiation can support varied uses but in an indirect manner. While walls typically meet at corners, spatial complexity seeks to open them up, thereby allowing for privacy while giving the opportunity for light to extend between different spaces and generating the perception of expanded spatial depth.

With the increased density of cities around the globe it has become a greater challenge to offer views from residential units beyond that of neighbouring buildings. The ability to have windows looking on to anything other than the immediate scene of the city is a challenge for the majority of urban dwellers. Spatial complexity reconsiders this common dilemma by challenging the use of windows and views to be increasingly diverse. One possible method of achieving this heightened diversification of views lies with the use of mirrors. Mirrors, of course, have long been used in interiors but have seldom been deployed in relation to mediating between interior and exterior. An exception is the Das House by Atelier Bow Wow in which windows and mirrors are tied together to reposition views. Mirrors are placed on angles strategically outside certain window apertures to reflect certain views and project more natural light into the interior. The result is an interior in which some windows and views operate conventionally while others use reflection to show other views such as the small Zen garden that sits at the base of the house. Through this technique a small site becomes bigger.

Cross Programming

> For if architects could self-consciously use such devices as repetition, distortion, or juxtaposition in the formal elaboration of walls, couldn't they do the same thing in terms of the activities that occurred within those very walls? Pole vaulting in the chapel, bicycling in the laundromat, sky diving in the elevator shaft?[6] —Bernard Tschumi

Cross programming is a strategy of overlaying multiple activities or programs onto one physical space. It does this by approaching the relationship between form and function as indirect; that a well-thought out formal configuration can support many different programmatic activities. To achieve its results it relies in part on the preceding strategies of hyper efficiency and spatial complexity. In an interior defined by cross programming the same space may be the home office, the bedroom, and even the washroom.

While cross programming is useful in realizing the full potential of the small unit, it is vital to extend this strategy beyond the unit interior. To fully achieve the possibilities of the small unit it is important that the overall building design consider cross programming. Circulation space, for instance, should be considered as a cross programmed social space and calibrated accordingly to support and enhance an array of social functions.

Conclusion

Hyper efficiency, spatial complexity, and cross programming are a set of design strategies that are particularly suited to the spectrum of contemporary social housing in which small units predominate. While maximizing the small unit's functionality, these strategies also serve to enhance the emotional, psychological, and physical needs of social housing residents. The serious consideration of these strategies provides exciting opportunities to expand upon and adapt them in relation to economic, site, client, and tenant specificity. Through an engagement with *small moves* social housing may find exceptional possibilities within its modest means.

1. Manuel Gausa et al., *The Metapolis Dictionary of Advanced Architecture* (Barcelona: Actar, 2003), 283.

2. Ralph Erskine quoted in- "Ralph Erkskine," *Times Online*, 19 March 2005.

3. Martha Stewart quoted in Brendan McGetrick ed., *Content* (Koln: Taschen, 2004), 224.

4. Aranguren Gallegos quoted in Josép Lluís Mateo ed., *Global Housing Projects: 25 buildings since 1980* (Barcelona: Actar, 2008), 150.

5. Kathleen Dorgan and Deane Evans, "Mainstreaming Good Design in Affordable Housing," in *Expanding Architecture: Design as Activism*, eds. Bryan Bell and Katie Wakeford (New York: Metropolis Books, 2008), 149.

6. Bernard Tschumi, *Architecture and Disjunction* (Cambridge: The MIT Press, 1996), 146.

THE POLITICS OF
SOCIAL HOUSING 2
JANUARY 26, 2009

A discussion between graduate students and guests.

GUESTS

Karen Stone, Executive Director, BC Non-Profit Housing Association

Cameron Gray, Managing Director, Social Development, City of Vancouver

STUDENTS

Magali Bailey, Rebecca Bateman, Bryan Beça, Maranatha Coulas, Stephanie da Silva, Idette de Boer, Anya Georgivejic, Andrea Hoff, Meghan McBride, Rodrigo Ferrari Nunes and Matt Purvis.

PROFESSOR

Matthew Soules

DISCUSSION

. . . .

Soules   **When you look at the government funding of social housing over time it appears to migrate across different populations, from seniors to families to the hardest-to-house. What are your thoughts about the factors that drive this migration?**

Stone   It's very hard to predict political will. A lot of it is driven by public awareness because the minute an issue becomes very prevalent in the media, like homelessness, you'll notice that the government's infusion of funding towards that issue does increase. This is unfortunate because ideally you would like to see your government serving you in a more strategic and long-term way.

And looking at homelessness—let's not deny the fact that the Olympics are a great incentive to help clean up the streets. I say that facetiously, but it is a motivator. What's going to happen after the Olympics is a concern. We've seen this in every country that has had an Olympic event—the great infusion of infrastructure prior to the games and then maintaining it afterwards is complex. My sense is that there's definitely a need for advocates to constantly be out there looking at projections and working with the government's policy arm. That's how we're operating. We want to make the longer term plans and then try to get government to buy into them as opposed to just waiting and getting the government to act. This is a bit of a shift. Maybe answering your question in five years time I might have a different answer. My sense is that policy is mainly driven by economics and how public an issue is.

Bailey   **Some of your organization's members own their properties outright. Are those housing co-ops? What's the incentive to remain not-for-profit?**

KS: No, co-ops are administered under another umbrella organization similar to ours. The incentive is the mandate of the organizations. Their missions and mandates are to provide affordable housing in their communities. When their operating agreements with the government expire they continue to offer affordable housing because that's what they're created to do. It's probably a better system than having government operate affordable housing because your local community based organization is comprised of a board of representatives who are really close to that community so they know what the needs are and they can drive the agenda of the community.

I would say with a very strong sense of righteousness that you can trust the non-profits as they've been delivering housing for years. They know what they're trying to achieve and they're trying to do it better and in increased numbers. They're not ones to lose units of housing. That's not to say that it doesn't happen. It's happened once in the last ten years—where an affordable housing project was sold off to create some revenues for the society to do a different piece of service delivery—but it's not common. We're confident that the non-profit sector will continue to expand on its mandate.

We've got folks sitting on $7 million worth of land in one particular community but they can't get development funds from the government because they want to build family housing. In the past if you had $7 million worth of land the government would jump all over that. But now, because the government priority is homelessness or the hardest-to-house, they can't move that development forward. They're forced to look for the money elsewhere. I think that shows you the level of commitment. These folks are really committed to making sure that housing expands and the number of units increases.

| McBride | **With the growing number of seniors, we may be approaching a crisis with regards to the provision of housing for seniors. Can you address that?** |
| Stone | The problem is not with the non-profits. It's with accessing the money to fund seniors housing. The government currently emphasizes the hardest-to-house and the seniors that fit that category are getting housing. Developments that are specific to seniors, ones that look at how someone can age in place for instance, are not sufficiently funded. |

It's not that the government doesn't acknowledge the need for more seniors housing. The issue is that within their present delivery model they have not sufficiently focused on seniors.

| Soules | **How do you see the role of architecture and architects?** |
| Stone | One of the things that frustrates me is that we're going smaller and smaller with unit sizes but we're not looking at the long term sustainability of the space. What happens if someone is healthy now and they can fit into the space, but they get older and a wheelchair is needed? What happens when they can no longer reach the cupboards that were built because they are too |

high? How about a person who is single but then finds a partner and maybe they have children? How will we build units that can expand and don't necessitate having to break down a wall and result in a unit that has two kitchens and two bathrooms? These are questions that I think could be thrown right back to the class.

Purvis **In your experience of working with non-profits have you ever seen a good example of an organization that is housing the homeless, then moves them to transitional housing, then to more long-term housing?**

Stone There are many non-profits who have a diversified portfolio. The one thing that I haven't experienced is a scenario where the need for the homeless shelter has diminished and then they can convert that space. I've seen non-profits that have started with a homeless shelter, have recognized the need for the next level, and then built second stage housing. The need for second stage housing will never decrease because you've always got people flowing from the first piece.

You might have people moving through a continuum of housing but you still have people standing on the outside of each of those developments. I haven't seen a housing provider change its function. They've changed some of the demographics that they've served to meet the changing needs of their community. For example, the issue of women fleeing violence gets spoken about with providers who primarily offer family housing and don't consider these women as fitting the family housing model. In certain instances, women's advocates have come in and said, "this is a family—women and children," and then the non-profits expand to allow that segment of the population into their housing. Or you have immigrant organizations partnering with a non-profit and saying that they need housing for their specific immigrant population and then you see an expansion. I haven't seen any problem dry up.

Gray Typically what's happened is that service providers have moved into housing. For example, organizations that weren't originally into housing at all, like child-care providers and health-care providers. British Columbia, and particularly Vancouver, has the lowest number of shelter beds in all of Canada, substantially lower than any other jurisdiction, and that's because of the SROs. The SROs function as a privately run shelter resource. As that stock diminishes—both because of its age and the intensity of need—we're starting to create more shelter space than we've had before and reluctantly so because it is more expensive. Supportive housing is seen as a better alternative.

Collectively we're being as cheap on the shelter end as possible. In the next twenty years we will never be in the shelter surplus position. There's just no way—they're very expensive. We'll always have this push for more and more housing for people coming out of shelters—which is frankly the way to go. A room with a door is essential for the self-preservation of a person. People need to have a place to be on their own and shelters don't provide that. In Calgary, they want to reduce the number of shelters—almost by half. Activists call it the anti-shelter, anti-homeless plan. Calgary has gone the route of creating huge shelters—thousand bed shelters—and now they have many people who are stashed in shelters who are working but can't find housing. Our focus in Vancouver has traditionally been on longer term housing.

In terms of design, there are lots of people looking at modular or manufactured housing these days. And also the mix of uses in terms of social enterprise being mixed with housing. There's been a lot of thinking on those topics.

....

Soules **Can you talk a bit more about social enterprise?**

Gray Housing societies are starting to branch out into social enterprises. Here in Vancouver, the Coast Foundation has its landscaping company and the Portland Hotel Society has been perhaps the most involved with its Sunrise Coffee Shop and Potluck Café. In some of our buildings, especially the ones where the city requires retail frontage, we are starting to see a lot of the non-profits come to the table to do some kind of business.

....

de Boer **What is your opinion regarding rent supplements as an option for supporting families within market rental housing?**

Gray   They won't work. There are more three and four bedroom units in the city's social housing stock than there are in the private rental stock. The city's rental stock is really skewed to the single person household and the region's market rental stock is pretty thin, so there is nowhere for these families to go.

         There are independent living programs that provide vouchers for people with mental illness or HIV. They would work great if we had more support stock, as there is nothing inherently wrong with rent supplements. They are valuable programs as they meet different needs. The problem in BC, not just Vancouver, is that the supply of rental housing is short. So one of the crucial issues going forward is the future of market rental housing.

         Social housing needs to be seen in context of rental housing. It's just a form of rental housing that is supported by the government with a degree of control.

         Canada is running on empty when it comes to rental housing. If we lose it and don't start to build more, or reinvigorate the stock, the demand for social housing is going to be huge and will intensify the affordability crisis dramatically. Condos don't provide the same rental stability that purpose built rental housing does and there is no guarantee that current condo rentals will be condo rentals in 20 years from now. So the security of the rental housing stock is crucial for Vancouver.

da Silva   **What are your thoughts about the appearance of social housing?**

Gray   The outside has to look contextual and you have to convince politicians when they go inside that the units are not too big. It has to be small, basic, and look like modest housing—that's the priority.

         The interior design is important because you want tenants to feel at home, but you don't want the press to be asking questions about how much things cost. The deserving and undeserving is always an issue in the business of non-profit housing.

da Silva	**Where do you see opportunities for innovation?**
Gray	Experiments in housing are difficult. It's not like any experiment that you can just throw out. If you have to tear down a building, like Pruitt-Igoe—that's a notoriety that you'd like to avoid. So experiments in housing are always very constrained.

The development industry is extremely high risk. Developers make really good money, but when things goes off the edge they go broke. The same risk you find in market development you find in social housing—same issue—big bucks and if it goes wrong, it goes really wrong. So there tends to be a conservative approach to innovation.

But of course there are pressures for innovation that we're all facing—the green stuff, green roofs, and all that type of stuff that every building is going to be doing.

Experimentation in social housing is often driven by a cost minimization. It is all about what the operation costs will be. What's the cost benefit analysis? Whereas in the market sector, it is driven by whether or not there is a market for this.

Soules	**Can you talk a bit about unit size. How small can you go?**
Gray	Around 1995, the City did a draft plan for housing in the Downtown Eastside in which we did a consultation about unit sizes. We did full scale mockups and got down to 180 ft^2 for a self-contained unit. We found that people could be happy living in a 190-240 ft^2 room. We have done 180 ft^2 rooms in renovated SROs like the Granville Hotel. And the Pennsylvania Hotel has 200 ft^2 rooms that are bright and with a lot of glass.

You can't go too small. One reason why overly small rooms don't work is that people don't stay in them. There is not enough space for people to feel comfortable for an extended period of time, so they spend a lot of the day elsewhere. Two basic things that really matter: make sure residents have TV and free cable so there is something to do for an extended period of time and lots of glass for natural light.

In 2005, Vancouver City Council approved 320 ft^2 as the minimum bachelor unit size for new construction. This was partly because anything smaller than 275 ft^2 starts getting into custom furniture and atypical appliances. Any savings made by going smaller, you've just spent, and then you spend again if you have to replace them.

A question we keep asking ourselves is how many residents are really cooking? Regardless, residents prefer a full fridge, as they often like to buy in bulk and put things in the freezer.

Purvis   **Is shared common space ever a viable alternative to larger individual units?**

Gray   It has been. An example is the Lore Krill project. That was one of the trade-offs they made with BC Housing, smaller units for more communal spaces. It's a self-managed co-op in which they provide the social infrastructure and look after the spaces. The issue with communal space is oversight and management.

Communal spaces tend to be consolidated into locations where there's oversight and wherever the administration is.

McBride   **How do you position modesty in social housing?**

Gray   Will units get bigger? Really the key modesty aspect is size. The compromise is always between capital and maintenance. Ever so often people realize as projects age, that if only they had put in better stuff to begin with they wouldn't have to replace it. Will the units get bigger? I doubt it.

McBride   Maybe not necessarily bigger units, but I could imagine ways that the lives of residents could improve over the long term if modesty wasn't a primary factor.

Gray   Well, there's definitely a balance between modesty and green design in the current environment.

Will a tension always be there? Absolutely. Do people need to have ownership of their units? You bet. But sometimes in non-profit, that modesty requirement encourages tenants to move on. This is an issue in social housing.

HONOURABLE MENTIONS

B.R.E.A.D. (BUILDING ROOTED ENTERPRISE AND DWELLING)
CAITLIN BAILEY
MAGALI BAILEY

One of the defining aspects of homelessness is exposure; living life in full view. This scheme seeks to invent a type of unit that responds to this reality by offering an exceptional degree of protective privacy while maintaining visual connections to the exterior. The result is a modulated building exterior that expresses the seriality of multi-unit housing and is performative by offering specially framed views.

The ground floor is devoted largely to a community bakery and an eating area that opens up to the alley. This represents an important potential reinvention of this type of building's relationship to the alley.

UNIT INTERIOR

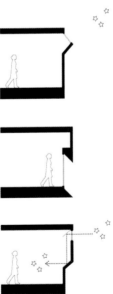

VIEW STRATEGIES

71

OPERATIONAL STRATEGIES

FRAME

The new addition (blue) frames the old structure. The existing heritage building becomes a building within a building, and a community within a community. This Russian doll effect is continued throughout by crossing many uses and structures.

CORE

The second step is to core the entire volume. This allows for better access for wheelchairs as it creates wider circulation. Wider circulation also mitigates altercations as one may keep a wide berth. Site lines are opened up to enable surveillance. Lastly, light is allowed to penetrate deep into the building and community is focused into the center.

EXTRUDE

All units are pushed towards the periphery. After years on the street, many people feel claustrophobic inside buildings. Invisibility is a privilege. The homeless spend all their time in full view. The units have been designed with a "privileged" view in mind. Every unit uses specific strategies to maintain a connection with the sky and the street without being seen.

CONNECT

The sound of water creates continuity throughout the building. The acoustic effect of falling water buffers noise and promotes a peaceful atmosphere. This shaft of water and light triples as the freight elevator. The sound of falling rain has also been exploited to reinforce the feeling that one is safe and protected.

ROOT

The building has at its heart a social enterprise. A commercial bakery provides opportunities for training and acts as an economic generator. It connects the building community to the larger community by serving those who remain on the street through the kitchen connecting to the alley behind.

2ᴺᴰ FLOOR

GARAGE DOOR FOLDS
IN HALF AND DOUBLES
AS COUNTER FOR SOUP
KITCHEN DISPENSARY

RUBBER RAMP FOR
BUGGY STORAGE

HERB WALL

COMMUNITY KITCHEN

BUILDING PANTRY
(SHARED)

TEACHING KITCHEN
/COMMERCIAL BAKERY

Baked goods
sold here

GROUND FLOOR

HONOURABLE MENTION
NEST
JORDAN LOCK

Supportive social housing units for the hardest-to-house are invariably small when compared to the vast majority of market housing. This scheme tackles this fundamental condition by maximizing the experiential potential of the small unit through planimetric and sectional offsets. Floors and walls within the unit shift in an interlocking relationship with neighbouring units and result in a variegated modular system. Each unit possesses a balance between an openness that allows natural ventilation and lighting and a differentiation of space that facilitates a diversity of function and an experiential expansiveness. The gently ramped circulation system assumes an almost topographical quality that is rare to this typology.

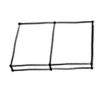  

UNIT INTERLOCKING DIAGRAMS

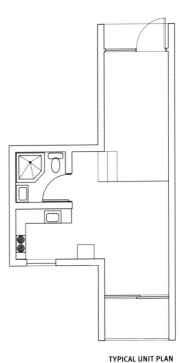

TYPICAL UNIT PLAN

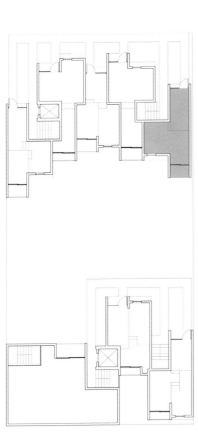

4ᵀᴴ FLOOR

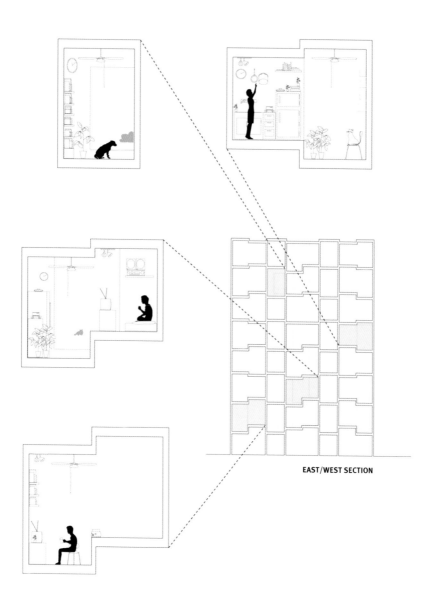

EAST/WEST SECTION

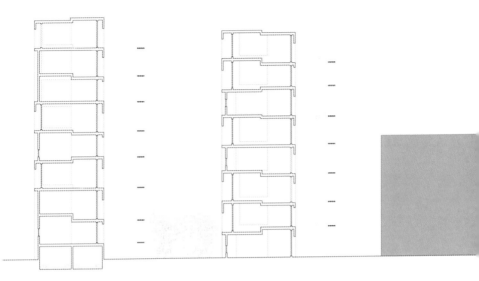

NORTH/SOUTH SECTION

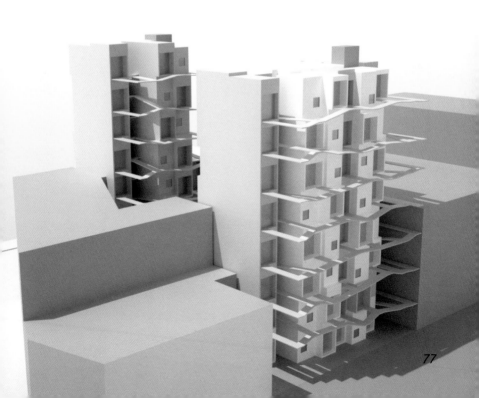

77

SELF-CONSTRUCTION
THE POLYVALENT ARCHITECTURE OF APPROPRIATION AND IDENTITY IN SOCIAL HOUSING
BRYAN LEMOS BEÇA

The lives of people identified as the 'hardest-to-house' are often defined by trauma, mental illness, drug addiction, and a discontinuous relationship with permanent housing that deeply affects their sense of self. It is possible for social housing that caters to this demographic to respond with design that enhances residents' self-identity. One such design approach can be called 'polyvalent architecture'—an architecture that offers a polyvalent framework for personal expression and the construction of identity. Such architecture stimulates the appropriation of space as a venue for expression. This appropriation enables the sense of ownership and pride necessary both to help establish a person's sense of self and to contribute to the enrichment of the public sphere to which they belong. Architecture that supports this type of identity construction relies on the careful treatment of dimension, materiality, and boundary conditions —polyvalent architecture has the greatest potential at the transitions between private and public. The boundary is where polyvalent architecture most effectively creates possibility and catalyzes action.

It is necessary to start by defining some key terms that will be used throughout the paper. Firstly, for the purposes of this exploration, *social housing* will be understood as including both transitional and permanent housing that ranges from supportive housing to public housing. It will not be used to identify emergency or transitional shelters. The reason for this more specific focus is that the acts of appropriation and expression which this paper is primarily concerned with require a length of stay longer than shelters typically provide.

A second term is *identity*. A typical dictionary definition of identity states that it is "the distinguishing character or personality of an individual."[1] Although identity is often thought of as being this simple, it is rarely so. Identity is unstable, and mobile. Everyone has multiple and "contradictory subject positions and are sometimes torn between identifications in different situations and places."[2] Identity in the public sphere for example, may take on a very different form than it does in private space. By necessity, identity is a flexible, fluid and mobile attribute. Identities are a process, a project, and sometimes, a performance.[3] In discussing identity, Richard Sennett refers to a quote from the psychologist Erik Erickson: "...an identity is the meeting point between who a person wants to be and what the world allows him to be."[4] In other words, there is an intersection of desire, and the imposed will of the public. This definition may be particularly apt when discussing the hardest-to-house who face severe public judgment, and who, by this definition, may be drastically limited in what they are allowed to be. In the context of this paper, identity will be all of the above: complex and multiple in its meanings, but critical to a person's sense of self and the projection of their presence in the world. Identity is closely linked with *expression*, which will be understood as the process of making one's feelings or thoughts and identity known to others.

The third and final term is *appropriation*, which will be understood as the act of taking something for one's own personal use. Where appropriation often has the connotation of being done without permission, in this case, permission will be assumed. Furthermore, appropriation will here refer exclusively to architectural space, and not to material goods or items.

Polyvalent architecture is a primary concern of Dutch architect Herman Hertzberger, who describes it as an architecture that "endeavours to offer a meaningful framework to the users, which they can 'claim' as their own and finish designing."[5] For Hertzberger, to 'finish designing' means to interpret and augment by taking ownership of and completing to one's own satisfaction. Along these lines architecture seeks to maximize possibilities of interpretation, use, and appropriation. As Hertzberger states, architects can design in such a way that "the result does not refer too outspokenly to an unequivocal goal, but that it still permits interpretation, so that it will take on its identity through usage."[6] In fact, a polyvalent design encourages appropriation. "What we make must constitute an offer, it must have the capacity to elicit, time and again, specific reactions befitting specific situations; so it must not be merely neutral and flexible—and hence non-specific—but it must possess that wider efficaciousness that we call polyvalence," says Hertzberger.[7] This statement is central to the idea of polyvalence; in order for the user to appropriate a space, its design must not be a blank canvas. Hertzberger argues that it is a prerequisite that the range of possibilities be graspable by the inhabitant; users must be able to draw on their own conscious experience to create associations with the space. The role of built form is to provide the groundwork for these associations to take place, so that the inhabitant can "compare them mentally with propositions of which he was already conscious or which can be raised from his subconscious experience."[8] In this way, a user can assess potential, and the space can become an "extension of [her] familiar world, and thus of [her] personality."[9] For the architect, this entails designing to evoke as many associations as possible; the more associations inhabitants can respond to, the more relevance the space will have for them, and the more they will be able to identify and appropriate the space for their own needs.

In what ways can polyvalent architecture accomplish this stimulation of appropriation? What operations can be undertaken to ensure an architecture with embedded potential? Dimension, materiality, and the design of boundaries are three primary considerations in making polyvalent architecture and will be analyzed in three projects: The Delftse Montessori School in Delft and the De Drie Hoven home for the elderly and disabled in Amsterdam, both by Hertzberger, and the Royal Hospital at Chelsea in London by Sir Christopher Wren. By focusing on dimension, materiality, and the design of boundaries in all three projects, the deployment of polyvalent architecture will be displayed.

The Delftse Montessori School, completed in 1966, encourages appropriation at thresholds by destabilizing the boundaries between public and private. In doing so, it stimulates the projection of individual and group identity from the private space of the classroom to the more public space of the shared circulation hall. The entrances to each of the 'L' shaped classrooms are situated within a small nook. These entrances function simultaneously as display spaces in which dimension is critical, as the careful measure of space produces in it the greatest number of possibilities and determines its accommodating capacity.[10] The window ledges above the entrances are deep enough to accommodate potted plants, books, models, clay figures and drawings. They function as 'open cabinets' that constitute a framework, to be filled in to the specific needs and wishes of the users. When filled, the entrance-way becomes personalized; the work and personalities of the students are displayed to the outside, projecting the identity of the classroom as a whole to the larger school. Instead of the boundary functioning as a barrier, it functions as an invitation for exploration while still providing necessary privacy.

Inside the classroom, a half-wall separates the entrance zone from the main body of the room. This separation articulates a space for smaller group work, while also offering a 'foyer' for those entering and exiting the classroom. The half-wall is topped with concrete blocks, a material that Hertzberger identifies as exemplifying the "reciprocity of form and usage."[11] Intrinsically, concrete blocks appear 'unfinished,' inviting further contribution from the inhabitants. Their hollow cavities can, for example, serve as storage or as a place to pot plants. While it is true that someone who wishes to pot plants will likely find a

Top **Delftse Montessori School**, Herman Hertzberger, Delft, Netherlands, 1960–1966.
Bottom **De Drie Hoven**, Herman Hertzberger, Amsterdam, Netherlands, 1964–1974.
Photographs by Herman Hertzberger.

solution for their needs regardless, the concrete blocks provide an incentive to be finished in this way. A clever use of materials that invite appropriation can enrich a space with its inhabitants' identity.

At De Drie Hoven, completed in 1974, Hertzberger expands on his ideas to create an architecture that uses subtle manipulations of form and dimension to encourage the appropriation of space. The resultant architecture breathes life into semi-public zones, with identity being expressed in a manner that enriches common areas. De Drie Hoven is a social housing project for the care of elderly and disabled people. The building consists of a number of long living halls with units that open on to an 'interior street.' As at Delftse Montessori, the careful articulation of thresholds is the catalyst for the claiming of semi-public space and the extension of individual inhabitant's identities into the public realm.

Individual units are coupled throughout De Drie Hoven's plan and share an entrance area in which each unit's door faces the other. This area is set back from the 'street' and demarcated by structural columns and a low wall that sits adjacent to each door. This approach creates two distinct but interrelated zones: the public zone of the interior street, and the semi-public zones of the entrance areas. The primary importance of the low wall resides with its dimension; it is modest in height but long enough to define the enclosed space as belonging to the unit. Its height and length establish a degree of privacy that precludes the overstepping of boundaries while maintaining a visual connection to the door. This generates a spatial gradient that frames the transition from public to private and is critical for invoking appropriation: the inhabitant must feel, to some degree, that it is their right to take over the space. In other words, the architecture must grant permission for its over-taking. As Hertzberger states: "Provided we incorporate the proper spatial suggestions into our design, the inhabitants will be more inclined to expand their sphere of influence outwards to the public area."[12] The intimate nature of this entrance area and its proximity to the entrance door encourage its take-over by the resident. This appropriation is also furthered by the deliberate location of the window, which allows each resident to keep an eye on their objects.[13] This is both a precaution against theft, and a reassurance of space. In this manner the user and the form reinforce each other and interact, a relationship that is akin to that between the individual and the community. "Users project themselves onto the form, just as individuals show their true colour in their various relationships with others...and thereby become who they are," says Hertzberger.[14] The furnishing of the space outside the unit extends the limits of the home beyond the front door and into the public realm, providing the public space with amenity and also projecting the identities of the inhabitants outwards. This projection is essential to our understanding of ourselves as our constructions reveal "how we desire to present ourselves to this world."[15]

Perhaps the most obvious and direct way to project identity is in person, from the individual body outward. At De Drie Hoven, the half-door is employed as a means of interconnecting the individual tenant to the larger building community. For Hertzberger, the half-door is a "distinctly inviting gesture: when half open the door is both open and closed, ... it is closed enough to avoid making the intentions of those inside all too explicit, yet open enough to facilitate casual conversations with passerby, which may lead to closer contact."[16] It provides a measure of privacy and security while maintaining openness and opportunities for expression.

The Royal Hospital at Chelsea in London is a retirement home for British soldiers who are no longer fit for duty or who have suffered debilitating injury. It was designed from 1682–1691 by Sir Christopher Wren and commissioned by King Charles II.[17] The building is comprised of a number of long wards that house individual units referred to as 'berths.' Each berth measures only 81 ft^2 and contains a bed, personal storage, and a study area while all other residential functions are communal.[18] Despite their modest size, the berths have a wealth of embedded potential in the way they interact with the larger community and facilitate appropriation and the projection of identity.

Much like the units at De Drie Hoven, the berths at the Royal Hospital face an interior street which contains common work spaces and gathering areas. The berth doors open onto the street, but when closed, form a long closed hall of solid wood. A fascinating projection of identity occurs with the provision

Royal Hospital Chelsea, Sir Christopher Wren, London, United Kingdom, 1682–1691.
Photograph courtesy of the Royal Hospital Chelsea.

of external coat hooks within the interior street. These hooks are used by the residents to hang their military coats and hats. The coats are particularly important for distinguishing rank, accolades, medals and tours of duty, creating an informative display of one's achievements and identity. To a large extent, the coats serve to tell the resident's biographies. Denis Diderot, the eighteenth-century French philosopher, hypothesized that "objects arranged within a space create a biography, or indeed autobiography, of the person who lives within that space, operating as words within a syntax, each word/object relating to the next to create a coherent whole, a life-story."[19] At the Royal Hospital, the berths are designed specifically to accommodate the telling of this story in a shared manner. The objects in people's lives create narrative, describe a relationship to home, and inscribe identity.[20]

The Royal Hospital at Chelsea also presents an incredible rich and variable threshold between the berth and the circulation hall. In an extension of the half-door's logic, each berth can open to the interior street in a number of different ways. Each has two large wood doors directly adjacent to each other, one of which is a half-door that has a built-in study attached to its interior face and the other a solid full-door. The combination of the single solid door and the half-door provide a number of possible permutations of public exposure. With both the single door and the upper half of the half-door open, the berth invites the community into the space. The resident can sit at his study to face the 'street,' or go about his business in his room while conveying that he is available for exchange. If the full-door is closed but the half-door open, the resident invites a certain degree of public interaction but maintains the spatial privacy of his domain. In a brilliant but simple move, the addition of a curtain that can slide across the eye-level of the study gives the resident the ability to make his berth available to the environmental benefits of the communal space such as air circulation and acoustic and olfactory connection while maintaining visual privacy. This polyvalent approach to the control of public and private space dissolves a boundary into a territory of potential social interaction where identity is projected and both the public and private realms have the opportunity to claim space within the other.

Of the three projects that have been discussed, none are social housing for the hardest-to-house. The school, the elderly home, and the veteran's hospital present, of course, distinct demands and requirements. What aspects of the design approaches exemplified in these three projects are applicable to contemporary housing for the hardest-to-house?

The importance of polyvalent architecture in the context of social housing for the hardest-to-house is reinforced with architectural historians Alison K. Hoagland's and Kenneth Breisch's observation that "while the distinction between image and identity can blur, the latter often takes the forefront in the struggle of minority or oppressed groups to exert their position in society, whether they construct this identity themselves or appropriate the place in which they find themselves, manipulating its forms and meanings to their own ends."[21] There is a real sense of urgency to catalyzing the appropriation of space at the service of bolstering self-identity for the hardest-to-house. Encouraging care and respect for the surrounding environment is essential to maintaining its function, particularly in the case of supportive housing which must often cater to persons who have may have experienced significant traumatic or suffer from mental illness. Appropriation can help inhabitants to feel as though they are needed, that the architecture requires their input in order to thrive. The ability to form an intimate relationship with a stable domestic environment responds to the upheaval, discontinuity and interruption many of the hardest-to-house have experienced for long periods of time. The ability to meaningfully store and display the objects with which they have developed relationships encourages the restructuring of Diderot's personal narrative. The ability to interpret space also gives the individual the power to choose, which in turn increases identity. This encouragement of self-construction, or in some cases, self-reconstruction, is an empowering tool that architecture can make use of in the design of social housing. It has the real potential to improve the quality of residents' lives.

While the overall qualities of the three projects that have been discussed are different than the reality of social housing for the hardest-to-house, all of their tactics can be calibrated and modified to suit specific contexts. The attention to dimension and materiality and the general diversification of key boundary conditions can be adapted to the needs of the hardest-to-house. While it may be unrealistic to expect the same degree of private property populating a semi-public area outside a unit as in De Drie Hoven, it is well within reason that strategically located windows, shelves, half-walls, half-doors, and engaging elements similar to curtains and concrete blocks can enhance and encourage personal identity and expression in a diverse array of housing types.

Homi Bhabha describes acts of boundary crossing as strategies of selfhood, whether those identities are singular or communal.[22] Hertzberger reinforces this concept by saying that "there is not a single relationship with which we as architects are concerned that focuses exclusively on one individual or on one group, nor indeed exclusively on everyone else, or 'the outside world.' It is always a question of people and groups in their interrelationship and mutual commitment... [I]t is always a question of collective and individual vis à vis each other."[23] By deploying tactics that enrich the crossing of boundaries through enhanced appropriation and identity construction, polyvalent architecture can help catalyze the strategies of selfhood that the design of housing for the hardest-to-house demands.

1. Merriam Webster Online, accessed Feb 19, 2009, http://www.merriam-webster.com/dictionary/identity.
2. Geraldine Pratt, "Grids of Difference: Place and Identity Formation," in *Cities of Difference*, ed. Ruth Fincher and Jane M. Jacobs (New York: The Guilford Press, 1998), 26.
3. Ibid, 28.
4. Richard Sennett, *The Fall of Public Man* (New York: WW Norton & Company, 1974), 107.
5. Herman van Bergeijk, *Herman Hertzberger* (Basel: Birkhauser, 1997), back cover.
6. Herman Hertzberger, *Lessons for Students in Architecture* (Rotterdam: Uitgeverij 010 Publishers, 1991), 152.
7. Ibid.
8. Ibid, 162.
9. Ibid.
10. Ibid.
11. Ibid, 168.
12. Ibid, 41.
13. Ibid, 40.
14. Ibid, 170.
15. Alison K. Hoagland and Kenneth A. Breisch, eds., *Constructing Image, Identity, and Place: Perspectives in Vernacular Architecture* (Knoxville: The University of Tennessee Press, 2003), xiii.
16. Hertzberger, *Lessons for Students*, 35.
17. Royal Hospital Chelsea website, accessed February and March 2009. http://www.chelsea-pensioners.co.uk
18. Ibid.
19. Eleanor Quince, " 'This scarlet intruder': biography interrupted in the Dining Room at Tatton Park Mansion" in *Biographies and Space: Placing the Subject in Art and Architecture*, ed. Dana Arnold and Joanna Sofaer (New York: Routledge, 2008), 55.
20. Ibid, 58.
21. Hoagland and Breisch, *Constructing Image*, xiv.
22. Homi K. Bhabha, *The Location of Culture* (London: Routledge, 1994), 2.
23. Hertzberger, *Lessons for Students*, 12.

INSIDE HOUSING FOR THE HARDEST-TO-HOUSE
FEBRUARY 9, 2009

A discussion between graduate students and guests.

GUESTS

Bill Briscall, Communications Director, Rain City Housing.

Earl Crow, Resident of Pennsylvania Hotel.

Judy Graves, Outreach Worker, City of Vancouver.

STUDENTS

Magali Bailey, Rebecca Bateman, Bryan Beça, Maranatha Coulas, Stephanie da Silva, Idette de Boer, Anya Georgivejic, Andrea Hoff, Meghan McBride, Rodrigo Ferrari Nunes and Matt Purvis.

PROFESSOR

Matthew Soules

DISCUSSION

Soules	**Earl, what do you think of the Pennsylvania Hotel?**
Crow	The Pennsylvania is great for me. I can chill out and write, I know people, and I'm comfortable down there. I like it. It has dignity and respect.
Soules	**What do you think is important for design?**

Crow	You got to make buildings bug-proof. The furniture people bring in is a vehicle for transmitting bugs all over the city. At the Pennyslvania, they bought furniture for the residents that would be hard for the bugs to live in. Great!
Graves	Being easy to clean is a big issue. People have no money for a vacuum bag, vacuum cleaner or plastic bucket. A mop is a luxury.
Crow	There are 16,000 residents in the Downtown Eastside and 6,000 of them use a needle every day. That doesn't include the ones who chase the dragon, the alcoholics, and the pill poppers. About 13,000 use an illicit drug every day. They are using money for drugs. If you are a woman, you are in the sex trade, and if you are a man, you are stealing. To go buy cleaning supplies or a hit of heroin; the cleaning supplies won't happen.

Beça	**What are some of the effects of hunger that you see in the Downtown Eastside?**
Graves	There are two research projects currently happening in the Downtown Eastside in which food service is introduced into buildings where it wasn't before. The research tracks the number of police calls before food service is introduced and the number after. The calls drop radically when people get food regularly. Almost all behavioral chaos in the Downtown Eastside is caused by low blood sugar. You are cold, you're dirty, you're wet, you haven't slept, and you get a donut and your blood sugar goes way high. Then it crashes and you are going to fight. A drug user with no food is erratic. A drug user with food is no more erratic then you or I. You wouldn't know it was the same person. The difference is food.

Soules	**Could you talk about what kind of shelter strategies you have witnessed homeless people using?**
Graves	Oh, the strategies for housing are unbelievable! Everybody has his or her own idea of "safe." If you are living on the street you are constantly getting beat up. It happens often. You wouldn't believe how many times people from a neighbourhood like Kitsilano go to the Downtown Eastside, get drunk, and beat people up in the alleys. Earl's friend was sleeping in a sleeping bag with his

wife when somebody poured lighter fluid on them. The sleeping bag melted to them. The man died and she is badly scarred. Now people don't zip up their sleeping bags for fear of being trapped.

For safety, people often sleep in stairwells, sometimes up emergency exits, and with dogs. People sleep in other people's cars. A lot of cars are left unlocked so that the windows won't get broken. A lot of people sleep during the days because it's safer.

Crow   I used to live in a tent in Crab Park. I'm well known in the Downtown Eastside, so I'm well protected. Nobody put their hand up in grade seven and said I want to be a prostitute drug addict.

Are you building this for you or for them? What pisses me off is the person who comes down at Christmas and hands out a sandwich. If you are doing it for yourself, then you can't look at yourself in the mirror. There's that balance of good and evil in all of us.

Just remember, skid row is a place in your mind, it's not a place in your city.

Crow   **Bill, what's the rate of violence at the Vivian building your organization, Rain City Housing, runs?**

Briscall   I know there has been some difficulty with some of the johns, but amongst the women it has been pretty good.

Crow   I know what sex trade women addicted to heroin are like and if you put them all in the same room, it would be difficult. Is the turnover very large?

Briscall   Not really. When we opened the project, we didn't really know how we were going to approach things and the turnover was quite high. Over the first two or three years the average turnover was four per month. But it stabilized. I was afraid we wouldn't be able to take anymore people. It gave people a chance to sit still and reflect and get ready for other housing.

Crow   Is there guidance for people who want to go to detox?

Briscall   Yes, there is. But you go to treatment for three months and then what? Come back to the Downtown Eastside and start using again?

Crow   Treatment is 30, 60, or 90 days, but the work is for the rest of your
            life. People need life skills. They need both detox and treatment.
            Donald McPherson wrote the paper about the four pillars approach,
            and there are some pillars missing. You need to follow up on these
            people. Once you put somebody in housing, well okay, but let's get
            them out of drugs and into some life skills and a job.

Briscall   Many people that come into housing go through culture shock.
            They aren't used to the daily tasks of living. Many say "fuck this,"
            leave and don't come back. This could be mitigated with more
            support staff. Some others are used to nomadic patterns and will
            just keep moving.

Graves   Many people living on the streets have a history of being moved
            from foster care to foster care. They can live in hell for ever. It's
            when things get good; a nice place to live and a good relationship,
            that they get terrified that they will lose this. It's called attachment
            disorder. We should never create transitional housing because it
            just reinforces the pattern of building relationships and breaking
            them. We need to build real housing and allow people to move
            through it if they need to.

Briscall   The term transitional housing gets redefined and redefined, over
            and over.

Graves   It would be nice if we could find a third word, because transitional
            is a scary word. Many people on the street were military kids and
            were moved so much. It's easy for them to let go, because that is
            their pattern.

Crow   It didn't matter where I was or the relationships I was in. I'd just
            walk out the door and that would be it.
....
Soules **Bill, can you describe life in the buildings you have worked in?**

Briscall   Situations vary, but back to survival behaviors, if somebody needs
            something now, they are going to let you know they need it now.
            Violence is usually not based on an attitude but if a mental illness
            has gotten to a point where the person is not thinking straight.

Soules   What do people want?

Briscall   It varies. They may be asking for coffee or other basic things. Bed
            bugs are a major problem.

Graves	It's like parenting. It's about teaching life skills without being condescending.
Briscall	A lot of what I learned parenting applies directly to my work.

da Silva **What is the typical process to get into social housing for the hardest-to-house?**

Crow Drugs trump everything for people in the Downtown Eastside. People prefer to live outside because of the conditions in the hotels. The conditions are so bad it's no different from living in the back alley. Plus you can't get into a hotel anyways.

Graves There are currently 1000–1500 people who want to get into some form of housing.

Crow You can't even get a box in the back alley anymore, none are vacant.

Briscall As an example, The Vivian, Princess Rooms, and two other buildings in the Downtown Eastside manage a single list of people trying to get housed. People move up the list according to need.

To go back to the bed bug stuff, we have a secret weapon. We are building a bed bug sauna. The sauna heats up to 60 degrees celsius and furniture and possessions go in there for two to three hours to kill everything. It's a prototype and if it's successful BC housing wants to put them in all 12 sites that are currently being planned for supportive housing.

Crow You wouldn't believe how many cockroaches live in a TV or in a toaster. They love electrical utilities. Hundreds of them!

Nunes **From what I gather, there is not a lot of hope, so to speak, for residents of these types of buildings to come out in a better position than they came in.**

Graves It depends. Often when people come into housing they are so close to death that the transition is going to be feet first. A huge number have AIDS and are not receiving treatment, hydration, or nutrition. If they can get into housing they may receive medical treatment but it may be too late. If someone can get into a place with kindness and respect and a washroom they may not need to move on. A person really engaged in their addiction may not want more than that.

On another note, a huge thing that is not talked about enough in regards to the Downtown Eastside is the prevalence of brain injuries—as a result of Fetal Alcohol Syndrome or accidents. Addictions are often subsequent to a head injury and there is no treatment that is targeted to this. Seat belt legislation has resulted in a lot of people surviving car accidents and ending up in the Downtown Eastside with a head injury. Suspicion is that it may be as high as 50-60% of people on the street that may have acquired or have been born with a head injury.

But back to your question, an example is the Granville Hotel that has 200 ft^2 rooms with a bathroom. They have 83 rooms and 137 people on the wait list. In that building there is some turn over of people moving on to a better life. They come in, lick wounds from the trauma of the street, and then move onto better housing. They move on to a 400–500 ft^2 unit, and further stabilize, and go back to work. But this is not the majority.

Briscall   60% of the people are in a revolving door and will end up back on the street.

Crow   If you have a relationship, you have a job, kids, and then you don't have that anymore, and you find yourself in the Downtown Eastside; you've lost everything. You may not have been a drug user, but you've given up. These people need to be given the opportunity to be empowered again.

Graves   Ideally people wind up in a building that is supported by staff who really understand the issues. The best thing is to get them in with an honest landlord. The required support services are so diverse that it's often better to bring the services into the building as needed. One resident might need a senior's addictions counsellor, another might need a youth addictions counsellor, and so on. One of the worst things is to have nurses in a building because their whole training is to invade people's boundaries. People will never feel at home because nurses are constantly overstepping boundaries. It is not a hospital ward, it's housing.

Briscall	BC housing more often than not decides to fund more housing, but what we really need is more money for support services in existing housing.
Graves	The hardest thing about working in the Downtown Eastside is working between a psychotic person and the psychosis of the system. If you take somebody for breakfast, it takes them an hour to eat because they are in so much dental pain. All the teeth are rotted off at the gum line. We can't take them to get a job because they have no teeth.
Crow	You know, at the Pennsylvania, I still sleep on the floor in my sleeping bag.
Graves	People coming in off the streets don't like overheated environments and they can't get used to mattresses; they rather a hard surface because that's what they are used to. Buildings often hire a community worker to create a community. But homeless people already have community! What if I asked Earl to ask 50 of his friends to move into a building, they don't need a community worker.

McBride **What are your thoughts about sizes of social housing units for the hardest-to-house?**

Graves	Most families in Vancouver don't have $400,000 to spend on anything. Most housing we are all living in is getting smaller. For housing the hardest-to-house we have to provide the basics people need to live in dignity. For instance, a place to put a TV set and a type of space where you don't have to start your day fighting with other people. I don't think anybody should advocate a 600 ft² unit unless they have moved a hoarder out of a 600 ft² unit. We have to design for the needs of the individual. Everybody has their own perceived need.

Coulas **We tend to speak a lot about the unit, but I'd like to know about the spatial needs of the entrance spaces and the transition spaces.**

Graves	What people really loved about old houses were their big old porches. A big front lobby with plate glass windows and beside or behind it, a beer parlor—that's an urban equivalent. People still

97

need that. It's done really well at the Veteran's Memorial Manor. The Triage building is not bad. There is a courtyard so people staying at the shelter can go right to the shared space with no bottle neck and it's easy to move about. Princess Rooms also has balconies on the front. In small towns people watch each other's cars all the time. In urban poverty people watch each other all the time. If people can't watch each other, there is anxiety. I think it's good to have a huge main floor space for people to watch each other. It's good to allow people to monitor each other for changes, anxieties in the street, shifts in behaviour, and the availability of food.

Crow   I don't do that, but yeah, I know people do that.

Briscall   We have cameras monitoring all of the entrances to suites and our residents feel happy about the cameras. They feel safer with more cameras.

Graves   Exactly, they love it. Something else I would add would be a large clock and an electronic calendar. The only clock in the Downtown Eastside is always wrong. Everybody in the Downtown Eastside is using this clock to get to their appointments! It's like a cultural artifact that describes the cultural dysfunction of the neighbourhood! You are really disoriented. Most people have had their watch stolen. Most people don't wear jewelry because it makes them a target. You can buy anything for $10 because that's the cost of a hit of heroin. Time should be built into the buildings, big and visible. Signage should be huge.

    Sound mitigation is probably the most important thing in design because a large number of people with mental illness are super sensitive to sound and produce a lot of very strange sounds.

Crow   A great thing was to put the waterfall in the Portland Hotel building. They found that the sound of running water smoothed everything out a lot. It calmed the hostilities of some people. There is a large aboriginal community, so murals are important in depicting aboriginal spirituality.

Graves   Often people think that poor people have less clothing than others. That's a major misconception. Shelving is very important.

SELECTED ENTRIES

HOME GROWN
AMBER BRUCE
SOPHIE MacNEILL
MORGAN WALLACE

The compact and efficient block of units at the north end of the site allows for the generous collective programming of the remaining area. The sloped glass roof that spans from the heritage façade to the two-level podium encloses a remarkable dining space with minimal effort. The relationship between this space and the roof-patio is provocative.

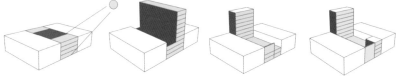

SOLAR DIAGRAMS

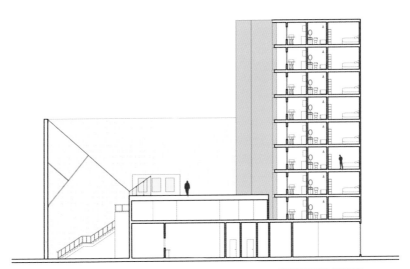

NORTH/SOUTH SECTION

3RD FLOOR

GROUND FLOOR

THE EMPOWERED LIVING PROCESS
STEWART BURGESS

Instead of proposing a specific fixed building design, this scheme offers a building strategy aimed at empowering tenants in the control of their living environment. Open floor plates embedded with a services grid provide a framework within which tenants construct their own units with set materials. A form of facilitated self-governance is envisioned to control building form and use.

UPPER FLOORS
PRIVATE
RESIDENTIAL

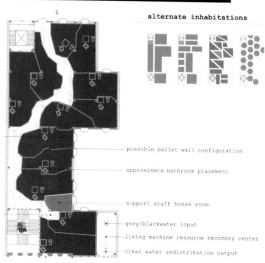

alternate inhabitations

possible pallet wall configuration

approximate bathroom placement

support staff break room

grey/blackwater input

living machine resource recovery center

clean water redistribution output

GROUND FLOOR
PUBLIC
COMMUNITY/
PRODUCTION SPACE

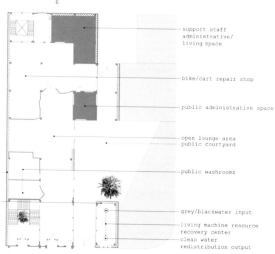

support staff
administrative/
living space

bike/cart repair shop

public administrative space

open lounge area
public courtyard

public washrooms

grey/blackwater input

living machine resource
recovery center
clean water
redistribution output

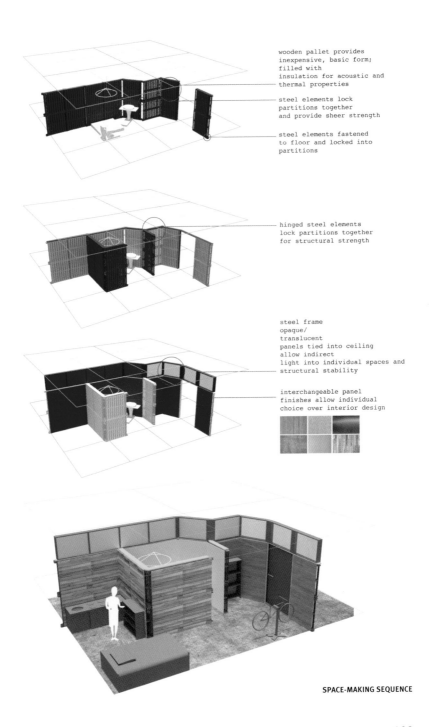

wooden pallet provides
inexpensive, basic form;
filled with
insulation for acoustic and
thermal properties

steel elements lock
partitions together
and provide sheer strength

steel elements fastened
to floor and locked into
partitions

hinged steel elements
lock partitions together
for structural strength

steel frame
opaque/
translucent
panels tied into ceiling
allow indirect
light into individual spaces and
structural stability

interchangeable panel
finishes allow individual
choice over interior design

SPACE-MAKING SEQUENCE

103

TRANSITION SPACE
AIDEN CARRUTHERS
FEDERICA PICCONE
ELSA SNYDER

Arranged neatly into a 'C' plan around a courtyard, the building offers a range of exterior spaces for relaxation and recreation while deploying ambiguous boundaries between different zones in the hope of gently encouraging interaction between building users. The move away from fixed boundaries in favour of more open transitional thresholds occurs between interior and exterior spaces and within the interior.

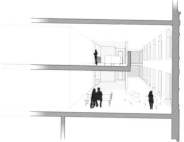

READING ROOM / COMMUNAL SPACES

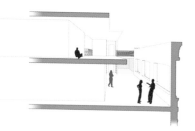

OUTDOOR CONTEMPLATIVE + CONVERSATIONAL SPACES

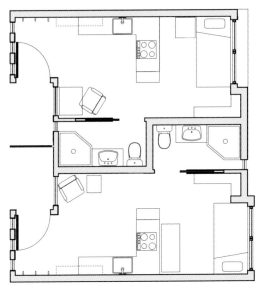

UNIT PLAN

PerF HOUSING
BROOKE DEDRICK
COURTNEY HEALEY
CHRIS SKLAR

800 ft² modules can be divided into two 400 ft² units or four 200 ft² units. These relatively simple and efficient modules are located along an open-air circulation system that facilitates the penetration of light and air, but perhaps most significantly attempts to recreate the openness and vitality of the street.

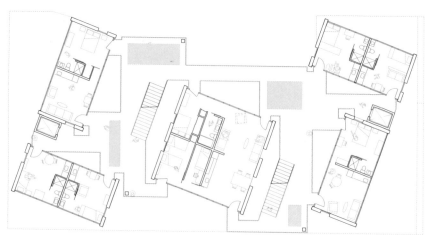

TYPICAL FLOOR

2 x 400 ft² RESIDENTIAL UNITS

4 x 200 ft² RESIDENTIAL UNITS

SOCIAL INTERCROPPING
ASHLEY GILBERT
ALICIA MEDINA

Urban agriculture is the primary agent for social integration and self-sustainability in this proposal. Food production space is dispersed throughout the building and even takes over the roof of the neighbouring Army & Navy building in an ambitious re-imagination of the possible future use of roofs in the city. Units are internally determined and arranged to facilitate the micro-commerce that proliferates through the entire project.

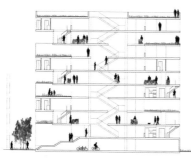

NORTH/SOUTH SECTION

EAST/WEST SECTION

108

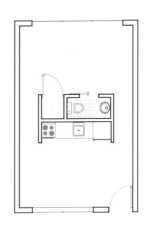

UNIT TYPE A

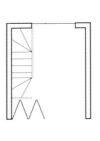

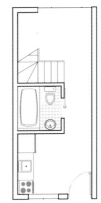

UNIT TYPE B

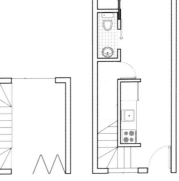

UNIT TYPE C

FUTURE SOCIAL
JONATHAN GRIFFITHS
BAKTASH ILBEIGGI

Concrete construction is deployed for durability and ease of maintenance, as well as for achieving an aesthetic permanence and strength be-fitting the program. Units are arranged into expressed clusters. Every third floor is an open space that permits a flexible interpretation of use over time.

Future Exterior

TYPICAL UPPER FLOOR

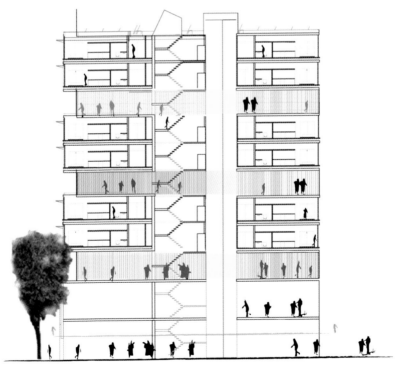

NORTH/SOUTH SECTION

SPIRITUAL HEALING 1990
MEHDI HASHEMI
SCOTT KECK

The 55 units, support service spaces, and commercial program that comprise this proposal have been organized into a series of discernable blocks that have then been consciously stacked onto the site. This results in an organizational legibility that can facilitate the establishment of certain types of communities. For instance, one community could appropriate a certain block as their identifiable 'neighbourhood.'

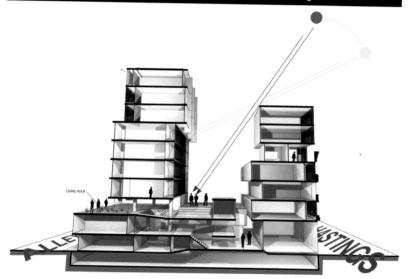

NORTH/SOUTH SECTION

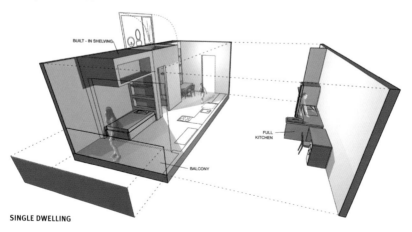

SINGLE DWELLING

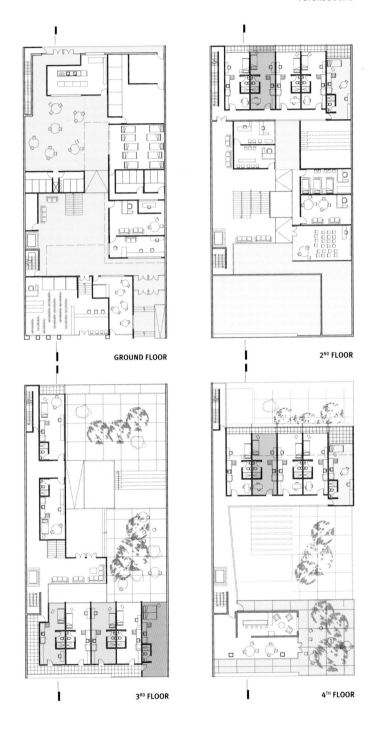

GROUND FLOOR

2ND FLOOR

3RD FLOOR

4TH FLOOR

OPEN HOUSE
JOSH JORDAN
PHIL RILEY

Housing is arranged into a single curved bar that is elevated above a semi-public ground plane which connects Hastings Street with the alley. While certainly raising security and safety issues, the nexus of services and dynamic form at the base of this proposal represents a new type of supportive social space interfacing with both the street and alley.

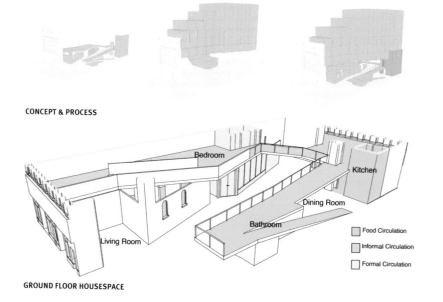

CONCEPT & PROCESS

- Food Circulation
- Informal Circulation
- Formal Circulation

Bedroom

Kitchen

Dining Room

Bathroom

Living Room

GROUND FLOOR HOUSESPACE

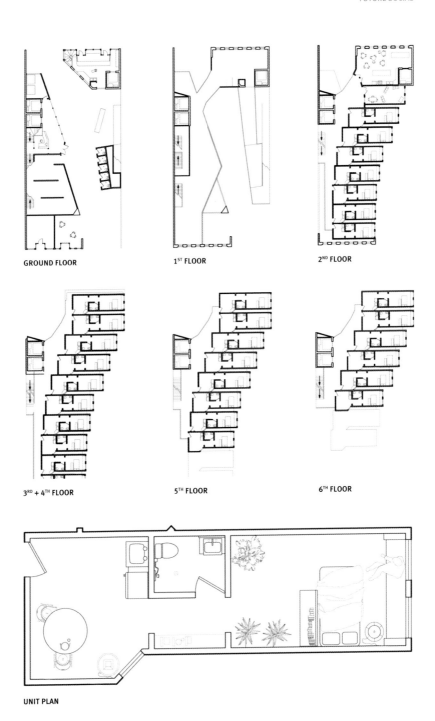

GROUND FLOOR

1ST FLOOR

2ND FLOOR

3RD + 4TH FLOOR

5TH FLOOR

6TH FLOOR

UNIT PLAN

BED BUG SOCIAL
CHRISTIAN KLIEGEL
KATY YOUNG

This scheme defies the constraints of the competition's site in favour of a parasitical network of living units that spread throughout the underutilized spaces of the neighbouroood; alleys, vacant lots, etc. The modular living units hang off existing structures or span across alleys and tap into existing services, thereby offering a contingent densification and intensification of use.

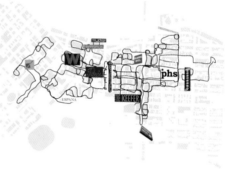

SITE CONTEXT

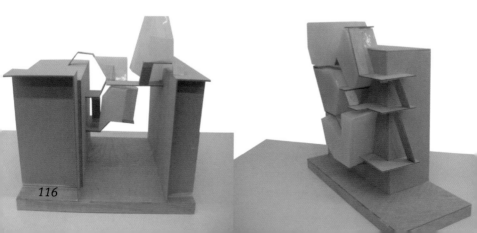

116

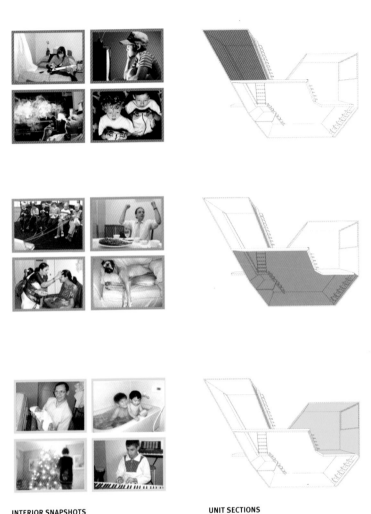

INTERIOR SNAPSHOTS

UNIT SECTIONS

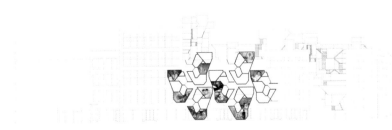

HASTINGS STREET BUILDING SECTION

117

DESIGNING SECURITY IN SOCIAL HOUSING
A THEORY OF OVERLAP
STEPHANIE DA SILVA

In the context of social housing for the hardest-to-house, establishing a sense of safety is arguably the most critical component in providing an environment that supports residents' progress towards independent living. Generating safety is more than just establishing security. It involves deploying architectural techniques that overlap the functions of a building and its security apparatus with qualities necessary in a place of healing and protective refuge.

As individuals who are transitioning from a life on the streets, the hardest-to-house often arrive in social housing with traumatic and abuse ridden pasts. Protection, security, and stability are privileges that most have been denied while living on the streets. Pressing issues continue to threaten the well-being of these individuals once they are housed. Psychologist Abraham Maslow's influential 'hierarchy of needs' places safety as its second most vital deficiency need, a need that when not met, increases anxiety and tension within any individual. If the mandate for accommodating the hardest-to-house is to help individuals progress on the road to independence, then it becomes ever more apparent that a critical role of architecture for this demographic is to generate a sense of safety.

In general, buildings often operate as filters that are constructed as a series of layers from least secure to most secure, or from public to increasingly private. In the design of a typical house, for instance, there are culturally accepted patterns of living that are manifestations of this progression—from the most public entrance foyer to the most private bedroom. Similarly, in facilities that house the homeless, there are architectural conventions that are fundamental to the creation of secure environments. Since supportive housing projects are often located in high crime areas that necessitate a specific level of security, buildings typically incorporate a security gradient through the use of physical barriers, networked technologies such as surveillance cameras, and personnel oversight. Typical tactics that are based on surveillance and territorial defense include secure exterior walls, bars over glazing, intercom systems, magnetized doors with secure holding zones, a network of security cameras, security guards, and a primary reception station. As one moves to living quarters, a change in section situates the residential program above ground level, walls offer privacy for individual units, and the lock to the door of one's room provides a final degree of personal control.

Many of these security tactics can be somewhat sinister, however, as their semiotic content conveys power and control. Particularly, security tactics when deployed as an afterthought result in unsightly and intrusive devices that negatively impact the comfort of occupants. In homeless shelters, for instance, the security design that ostensiblty facilitates optimal operation often intensifies the anxieties of the homeless and goes against the goal of establishing a shelter as refuge. Common security tactics meet the requirements of a physically secure environment but do little to foster the positive spirit of the building community or the neighbourhood.

In the past, homeless shelters were often created by converting armory or warehouse spaces into endless rows of temporary beds. In addition to the use of security cameras, staff insisted on the need for clear sight lines and surveillance at all times. Unfortunately, "the often-massive shelter dormitories provided no such assurances [of safety] to their clients, and the residents saw the staff

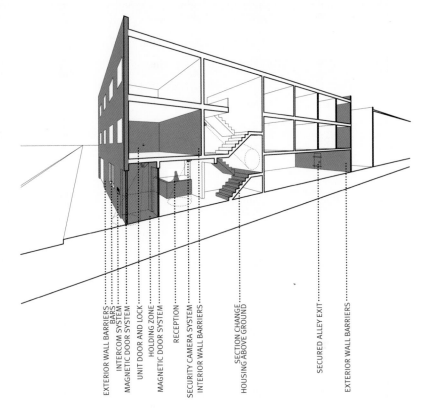

EXTERIOR WALL BARRIERS
BARS
INTERCOM SYSTEM
MAGNETIC DOOR SYSTEM
UNIT DOOR AND LOCK
HOLDING ZONE
MAGNETIC DOOR SYSTEM
RECEPTION
SECURITY CAMERA SYSTEM
INTERIOR WALL BARRIERS
SECTION CHANGE
HOUSING ABOVE GROUND
SECURED ALLEY EXIT
EXTERIOR WALL BARRIERS

BUILDING AS A FILTER: LAYERS

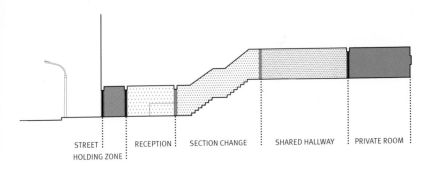

STREET
HOLDING ZONE
RECEPTION
SECTION CHANGE
SHARED HALLWAY
PRIVATE ROOM

SECURITY GRADIENT: UNFOLDED SECTION

as guards."[1] The apparent operational needs of these shelters conflicted with the needs of the population they served and the large, open spaces conveyed a crushing impression of exposure and vulnerability.[2]

Security through surveillance of the built environment is a topic of continuous debate. Jeremy Bentham's 18th century panopticon, a type of prison in which the design regulates prisoner behaviour by ensuring their perception of continuous and omnipresent surveillance, has proven a timeless conceptual and operative diagram. Michel Foucault invokes this architectural construct in *Discipline and Punishment* as an analogue for modern 'disciplinary' societies and their pervasive inclination to observe and normalize. Similarly, in his canonical novel, *Nineteen Eighty-Four*, George Orwell describes a society where everyone is under complete surveillance by the authorities, mainly through telescreens, through which people are constantly reminded by the phrase "Big Brother is watching you." Whether or not one is actually being watched, the architecture and technologies of 'surveillance' convey a sentiment of invisible omnipresence. While surveillance can have good or at least neutral intentions behind it, its processes and practices also imply that individuals are not to be trusted. Surveillance, in this sense, supports suspicion. Security guards, surveillance cameras, and other devices, including physical barriers, inherently maintain a hierarchical relationship between those who are in control of them and those who are not. The necessary negative effects accentuate social inequality and signal a decline of trust in social relations.

In a sensitive environment like supportive social housing, these tactics are questionable and can be unwelcoming. The semiotics of security, if left unchecked, create a sense of institutionalization. As American architect and academic Sam Davis states in regards to homeless shelters, this institutional character and omnipresent surveillance "inculcates a resistance to acceptable social behaviour to such an extent that the homeless either desperately avoid shelters or, once entering, create psychological walls (in absence of real ones) in order to achieve some degree of personal privacy."[3] The perception of various forms of social housing as institutionalized places can lead to the distressing choice by many to rather face the physical challenges of remaining on the streets.[4]

Creating a sense of safety is more than defining a physically secure environment. Certain techniques and tactics have the potential to provide security but in a way that also adds other values to their context. Particularly within social housing, architecture that establishes a sense of safety can be polyvalent, ensuring security and also helping to establish less tangible qualities like trust, friendship, reliability, and community. In this manner, a supportive social housing facility can become a refuge.

Security and Community

In *The Death and Life of Great American Cities*, Jane Jacobs suggests that crime can be reduced by placing "eyes on the street."[5] The thoughtful design of elements and spaces that generate a sense of community can replicate this idea of 'natural' surveillance at the scale of the building. For those in social housing, this has powerful implications, as it is a form of social control within a culture of surveillance that is not top-down, but rather, involves everyone as both the watcher and the watched. In an oddly democratic way, this natural surveillance encourages discipline and affects social control while instilling a sense of dignity.

The Dutch door is an excellent example of a multi-purpose element that is a protective barrier, community generator, and environmental modulator. As a simple device, the way it operates in a variety of ways to provide degrees of privacy and connection is compelling. As a door it facilitates access. With the bottom half closed, it provides a degree of security while retaining connectivity and enhancing airflow. Closed and locked, it provides heightened privacy and protection. Many projects in the past have had difficultly grappling with the same balance of security, community, and user comfort. Residents of New York City flophouses, a term given to describe residential hotels and lodging houses for the poor, were often subject to contemptible living conditions at the cost of attempting to engender privacy, control, and security. Residents described spaces as minimal dwelling units each with

... a locking door, but no ceiling; the top was roofed with chicken wire that kept out the 'crawlers' or 'lush divers' who might climb over the walls to steal the belongings of the sleeping or unconscious resident. The wire also kept people from occupying a cubicle without paying, and it provided a bit of ventilation and access (albeit minimal) to light.[6]

In contrast, the simple yet thoughtful design of the door can reinterpret a security element to be a polyvalent mediator of public and private within the building community.

Similarly, the design of personal space in a temporary or emergency shelter can be considered for its role in creating a safe and secure environment. Required is a degree of privacy within the functional layout of shelters, a place to secure belongings, and an expression of individuality while also establishing a sense of community. In the Contra Costa Shelter, Sam Davis designed a cabinet that addresses all these concerns. While each cabinet could not be unique because of costs, the design intends the device to be clearly associated with one individual in terms of proximity and orientation. In terms of providing a degree of privacy and security, the cabinets restrict views between beds and have lockable storage. Its form is a simple abstraction that appeals to the culturally coded notions of 'home.' The cabinets establish a collective presence. It is the form and its imagery that stands out rather than the individual beds.

Much like the front porches encouraged by Jacobs and the advocates of new urbanism, many social housing projects include front entrance 'living rooms' that offer a chance to relate to the community while monitoring neighbourhood activity and facilitating guest management. Judy Graves, a well known Vancouver outreach worker, states: "In urban poverty, when you can't watch each other, there is anxiety."[7] Front entrance spaces and other communal spaces, such as kitchens and dining rooms, provide a degree of security that overlap with opportunities for social exchange within the building.

Generating solidarity within social housing is imperative because as residents grow to depend on each other it permits the projection of reciprocity and kinship through time. The social obligation of kinship is more powerful

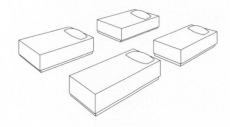

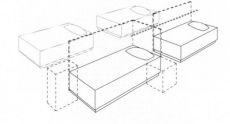

INDIVIDUALITY
    STORAGE
    HEADBOARD
    NIGHT STAND

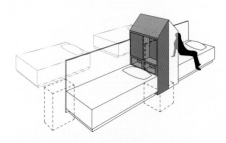

INDIVIDUALITY
    STORAGE
    HEADBOARD
    NIGHT STAND
PRIVACY
SECURITY
    LOCKABLE UNIT

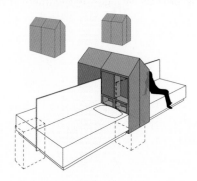

INDIVIDUALITY
    STORAGE
    HEADBOARD
    NIGHT STAND
PRIVACY
SECURITY
    LOCKABLE UNIT
COMMUNITY

DIAGRAM OF SPACE CHANGE WITH ADDITION OF PERSONAL CABINET

Insite, Sean McEwen, Vancouver, Canada, 2003. Photograph by Christoph Runne.

than what a technological device like a security camera generates. For most homeless, a supportive environment and a sense of belonging to a community is a much needed component of safety.

Security and Self-Dignity

At the scale of the room, the attention to layout and the use of specific materials can achieve security in a respectful manner. Insite, located in Vancouver's Downtown Eastside, is the first legally supervised injection site in North America. While cameras and security controlled doors are present, they are limited to the entrance and post-injection zones. There are no security guards in the facility. The creators of Insite were careful to respect their users, many of whom expressed concerns over being recorded while injecting. Within the 12-seat injection room, the incorporation of mirrors at each station replace the role of security cameras and allow medically trained staff to supervise without infringing on the privacy of users.

Russ Maynard, an organizer at Insite, argues that the primary strength of its security system is not in its formal techniques, but rather in the genuine human relationships between the staff and users.[8] Insite is often a user's first point of contact with health care professionals so instilling a sense of trust is important.

Insite recognizes this as an opportunity to build confidence with health care professionals. Within the facility they have designed a way of supervising that respects the people they serve while retaining security and control.

Security and Circulation

Traditional Hakka housing in Fujian, China, exemplifies a simple yet clever way in which a building's form serves as a means of protection and surveillance while also enhancing community interaction. Each ring-shaped building constitutes a self-contained residential village. Inward facing and closed off to the outside world, the communities of Hakka people could defend themselves against attackers and sometimes long drawn out sieges.[9] Double height family units form a ring around an open central community area. Living spaces and kitchen facilities are located on the ground floor while bedrooms and storage are located above. Family members can only access the rooms above from four stairs that rise from the central shared space. This means that an individual must always proceed from living spaces to bedrooms by crossing the public space. In this way, family groups have a heightened awareness of movement as the circulation provides a means of surveillance. Furthermore, the continuous movement through the shared central space creates opportunities for encounters and engagement that build relationships within the community.

A courtyard layout can be applied to the program of contemporary social housing to achieve similar qualities. Arranging units so that the every day use of circulation paths creates activity around a community focused centre encourages daily connection while enhancing security. Circulation becomes the buffer zone between individual units and the common courtyard.

Security and Beauty

During research for the design of Lu's Pharmacy for Women in Vancouver's Downtown Eastside, a project of the UBC School of Architecture and Landscape Architecture's community outreach program, students asked three women

Traditional Hakka Housing, Fujian, China, 12th to 20th century. Photograph by Ryan Pyle.

to capture with photographs their experience of existing pharmacies in the neighbourhood. The students were astounded when the participants returned with over half of their images depicting facades reinforced with security bars. Unsightly and unwelcoming, the presence of these bars conveyed a closed and distant attitude towards customers and the larger community.

As a response, the students pursued a different representation of security and what it can do. They designed a perforated metal security gate with an abstracted cherry blossom motif. When the pharmacy is closed at night and the security gate is extended into place, lights from the interior filter through the perforated screen. The security gate is no longer only concerned with defense; it is also about bringing beauty to the street.

Even within small increments, security features have the ability to extend into the realm of aesthetic enhancement. Roger Marvel Architects (RMA) was commissioned to reinterpret the Jersey barrier, a concrete barrier that regulates traffic, for New York City. RMA's design exploits the potential found in barriers and balances the contradictions of enhancing the vibrant streets of New York

New York Stock Exchange/Financial District Streetscapes + Security, Rogers Marvel Architects, New York, NY, 2003 – 2009. Photograph by Rogers Marvel Architects.

with installing integral public safety devices. The result is a set of traffic barriers that also act simultaneously as seating and visually attractive sculpture. A socially sustainable and cultural response to a mundane problem, the design and scale of the new security barriers adds diversified value to the community.

Security and Entertainment

Security overlaps with entertainment in Diller & Scofidio's exploration of display, surveillance, and control in *Facsimile*, their permanent installation at the Moscone Convention Centre in San Francisco. A 16 foot by 27 foot video screen moves along a horizontal tracking system attached to the façade of the building. Video cameras record real-time activity from within the building and broadcast the imagery, which is mixed together with pre-recorded fictional imagery, to the street.

This installation is a provocative consideration of surveillance technology that has ostensibly produced a more transparent world. While operating within the means of security, surveillance is here transformed into performance.[10]

The installation proposes an alternative language of security, one that addresses culture and entertainment, rather than only power and control.

In Vancouver, as in cities pretty much everywhere, there are sprinklings of the same idea. In the Cactus Club Café at the base of the Bentall 5 building, security is incorporated into the interior design as an element of pop culture. Three small flat screen televisions are aligned vertically in the elevator lobby and another series of screens are incorporated into the hostess stand by the entrance. The screens project live surveillance recordings of the restaurant in a manner that allows surveillance to function as a spectacle in which diners are both the watchers and the watched.

Conclusion

Security, a necessary and fundamental component of social housing for the hardest-to-house, challenges designers to be critical of its methods. In order to avoid the negative aspects of institutionalized environments, a distinction must be made for the particular sensitivities of the hardest-to-house. Housing for these people is more than a physical shelter from the elements. It is a place of healing. Instilling a sense of safety and trust is essential. Therefore, the perception of security tactics must be carefully considered. Often seen at odds with architectural production, security can be reconsidered in unforeseen ways that can create additional benefits for an internal building community and also the community at large. Community, self-dignity, beauty, and entertainment— these are only a few of the terms within which security can be repositioned for a more positive and polyvalent role. In social housing, where tight budgets and limited space often constrict design, polyvalence and multi-functionality are vital. Only when the role of security overlaps with the other values of social housing will security tactics effectively engender a sense of safety and refuge.

1. Sam Davis, *Designing for the Homeless: Architecture That Works* (Berkeley: University of California Press, 2004), 27.
2. Ibid, 27.
3. Ibid, 27.
4. Ibid, 27.
5. Jane Jacobs, *The Death and Life of Great American Cities* (New York: Modern Library, 1961).
6. Davis, *Designing for the Homeless,* 37.
7. Judy Graves. See the discussion titled *Inside Housing for the Hardest-to-House* in this book.
8. Maynard, Russ. Personal interview. April 15, 2009.
9. Herman Hertzberger, *Space and the Architect: Lessons in Architecture 2* (Rotterdam: 010 Publishers, 2000), 126.
10. Guido Incerti, Daria Ricchi and Deane Simpson, *Diller + Scofidio (+Renfro): The Ciliary Function: Works and Projects 1979 – 2007* (Milan: Skira, 2007), 166.

SERVICE DISCOURSE
MARCH 2, 2009

A discussion between graduate students and guests.

GUESTS

Janice Abbott, Executive Director, Atira Women's Resource Centre.
Darrell Burnham, Executive Director, Coast Foundation Society.
Liz Evans, Executive Director, Portland Hotel Society.

STUDENTS

Magali Bailey, Rebecca Bateman, Bryan Beça, Maranatha Coulas, Stephanie da Silva, Idette de Boer, Anya Georgivejic, Andrea Hoff, Meghan McBride, Rodrigo Ferrari Nunes and Matt Purvis.

PROFESSOR

Matthew Soules

DISCUSSION

Bailey	**Can you talk a little bit about social enterprise?**
Evans	Many non-profits are trying to get involved in social enterprise in order to help make neighbourhoods more livable. We have been trying to get cafés, washing machines, and grocery stores in place so that people can feel calmer and have an enhanced sense of place. What's needed is enterprise that is friendly to the low income community that can also be enjoyed by everyone else.

We operate a number of commercial spaces such as the Potluck Café in the Portland Building and the grocery store at the base of the Washington Building. I've been arguing that the City should reduce the rent it charges on the commercial space it owns, because it would be a huge benefit to the community if non-profits could operate some of those spaces.

Abbott   In the buildings where the City has retained control of commercial space, the reality is that it's often vacant. The City can't rent it out. I think it's much better that a non-profit puts something in. However, this is met with opposition from a variety of sources, such as the business improvement associations. At the Rice Block, one of our projects currently under development, we've created a 450 ft^2 storefront on Hastings Street that has a community kitchen behind it. The store will sell the products that are created through our alternative employment initiative: "Enterprising Women Making Art." The space is tiny but perfect for our first store.

Evans   The City tends to control commercial spaces with higher income people in mind. Their constituents bought low to sell high and don't give a damn about the rest of the community. But poorly dealt with commercial space makes things bad for everyone.

The fact that non-profit organizations have too often not been allowed to take on important services jeopardizes the viability of creating healthy neighbourhoods. It is short-sighted on the part of the City. Commercial retail space, as far as the City is concerned, requires money and activity only, and ignores all other social aspects of the operations. The City neglects questions of accessibility and quality of life for the underprivileged.

de Boer   **Jumping to another topic, what are your thoughts regarding materials in the types of buildings you operate?**

Abbott   Concrete works well as it is clean and unbreakable if properly built. Detachable furniture and other fixtures are problematic, as are un-reinforced walls that can be poked through easily.

Burnham   Making sure the buildings are secure is perhaps the most important thing. Everyone wants safety.

Abbott	We used plexiglass on some walls to allow children to draw. There are always new products that can be tried. But customizations have to be designed according to the particular needs of the people that we are intending to house.

We have to be careful with mirrors. People have broken them and got hurt. Blinds also get destroyed easily.

Evans	Putting blinds within glazing is a good strategy. There are also huge problems with curtains. Some of our residents like to be in the dark a lot of the time. Sometimes people feel safer in small areas surrounded by their belongings.

For residents who have experienced extensive trauma, often all you have to do is open the door to their room, to understand their emotional pain. The emotional chaos people feel is often expressed and reflected in how they live in their units. This makes standard designs less successful, and means that creating modifications is often necessary.

For example, we wanted to put people into rooms that had cupboards with doors, but they don't really work since the doors get broken and torn off. Hinges are also a potential liability as they easily break. Wood that is often used to make things aesthetically softer ends up covered in cigarette burns. Beds get torn off. Anything that can be torn off will be. It's a tough crowd.

Georgijevic	**Mixed tenancy, can you three talk about it?**
Burnham	There's a recently completed condo tower with a hotel and high-end restaurant at the corner of Robson and Richards Streets. The project also includes forty-five 350 ft^2 units of social housing that we are operating. Last week our tenants were being verbally assaulted by the rich people who paid about $700,000 for their units. They were unhappy that the poor are getting their units for $375/month. They harass the poor for the privilege of being there. But there's a really neat community within our group of units that is working quite well.
Evans	We were involved in the Woodward's project. We partnered with the developer, gathered petitions concerning the project, and generally thought a lot about many of the elements that are going

135

in. When the project opens we will be running 125 SRO units that will exist alongside the market housing. Getting these 125 units is good but the percentage of low income housing in the Downtown Eastside has decreased since the last census. Poor people need to be housed right away. We want to partner with developers and other non-profits to do this—it's not rocket science.

Having different socio-economic groups living together does raise issues. For instance, sometimes condo owners contest the right of a person to sleep on a public bench. People have to be educated on issues of homelessness, contested spaces, and rights to space.

Abbott	I live in a building that includes co-op artist studios and condos, so it is itself an integrated community that is also situated within a larger integrated neighbourhood community. Yet, after the City installed a bench outside the building there was a huge outcry to get it removed because some residents were afraid it would attract unwanted behaviour. Many people refer to homeless people who sleep on benches as indigent. Rising property values can cause trouble.
Burnham	What we are seeing is the use of the profits gained from the sale of condos to build social housing.
Evans	The government just needs to build the housing and forget about the market considerations. The amount of market housing that has to be built in order to supply the demand for social housing in the Downtown Eastside is just not achievable.
Soules	**Is it possible to answer this question: What is the optimal number of units in a building for the type of people you serve?**
Abbott	Some say 30 to 40 units if the residents are in high need. However, the reality is people just need housing, so anything you can get, you can make work.
Burnham	It's a function of staffing, size, location, amenity space, and mix of tenants. As a non-profit, if someone gave me a building with 200 units, I would think that it's too big. But we would figure out a way to make it work. We could layer the type of residents in such a manner that it would work.

Evans   Sometimes a smaller number of units in a building can cause problems. For example, one of our residents was a chronic vomiter who was considered impossible to deal with. Our philosophy and approach is about offering a therapeutic community. Hospitalization did not stop his vomiting, but when he was staying at the Portland he did stop. Then we moved him into another smaller building that we operate. Within two weeks he had assaulted two staff members and was vomiting everywhere. He couldn't cope with the level of scrutiny and intimacy he felt there. In this smaller setting his condition worsened, so it's not about size; it's about fit.

Abbott   One of our buildings has eleven units and it is very hard for the residents not to get involved in one another's life. In a larger building people can be avoided, but the smaller the building, the harder that gets. This closeness can create problems and much more work for staff, and make it less safe for a lot of people. A balance must be found between the numbers of residents and staff.

da Silva   **On fostering a sense of safety: We've heard about some simple examples that work—such as Dutch doors. Could you describe any other successful design solutions for creating safety that you have observed?**

Burnham   Gathering spaces are important. Especially gathering spaces that can be monitored from a distance and allow staff to have a sense of what's going on. They're good for getting to know people and quickly learning how people are doing. If something is not going well, you can figure out what is happening, and then develop an intervention if necessary. Weekly meals and gathering spaces are both very important.

    Guest management is also critical. Even if a visitor is safe, if residents see them as a stranger, it can cause issues. People with mental illnesses can be exploited; therefore staff need to oversee who gets into the building. Guests sometimes find ways to break into the system and stick around and cause considerable harm.

| Evans | At the Portland we have two doors with a man-trap in the middle, which help to control access to the building and keep dangerous individuals out. It's a huge success. |

Fire doors to back alleys should be kept locked and safe because people will try to get in any way they can.

Setbacks and articulation in the façade are themselves problems. The City is always asking for articulated facades but these are the places that people deal drugs in.

Beça | **Regarding the storage of personal items and identity: In which ways do people do that?**

Evans | People use all kinds of things to express themselves. One of our residents creates art work with garbage that he collects and has turned his unit into a gallery of his art. Some people have cats and take care of each other's pets.

Abbott | A lot of people we work with have never had anything, so they hoard stuff. It's a constant kind of give and take with who brings what into the building and how. We want to respect tenants' wishes but also ensure health and safety. There are issues with rodents and bed bugs. Everything you have, when you have little, becomes very valuable and personal and you are afraid to let it go.

Burnham | Though it's uncommon, we have had tenants keep rooms that are filled up from floor-to-ceiling with books. We had one resident who took us six months to work with to get his room clean and safe. We worked with a mental health team to figure out a specific strategy for him.

Evans | If you can pay residents money to clean up their room, that's a great incentive. It's a job that is more useful than pushing a cart around the street. Some of the rooms get horrific, and people keep all kinds of things imaginable.

Soules | **During this course we have often found ourselves having conversations that somehow revolve around society-in-general's non-acceptance of radically diverse ways of living. From an architectural standpoint, it seems to me that we are talking about making buildings that respond specifically for this other-ized homeless population, but the reality is that**

most buildings for this population basically operate like any other building. Of course, we don't want to stigmatize people and want everyone to be comfortable, but how can design possibly celebrate and cater to real differences? On storage and hoarding, for instance, are there less obvious architectural tactics that can meaningfully respond to these issues?

Abbott   A full on hoarder will pack every inch of their entire unit with stuff.

Evans   But in relation to what can be designed, our buildings are led by cost. There are modesty guidelines that the government imposes. We had to change the names of what we wanted sometimes to satisfy the guidelines. For instance, a hair salon for people who spend most of their time in Downtown Eastside alleys does not conform to the modesty guidelines. But we got one in the Portland. I find it really hard to not go crazy with these modesty impositions. Greenhouses and gardens, for instance, are very hard to get approved.

Nunes   Isn't that itself a form of stigmatization with these types of projects?

Burnham   Sure it is.

Evans   We encounter people who pay lots of money for their condos and resent poor people living well in their newly gentrified neighbourhood.

Abbott   We're dealing with taxpayers and government for whom it's hard to see poor people having anything other than a small rectangle to live in.

Burnham   There are maximums set by the government on square foot construction costs. You are looking at roughly $260–270/ft^2 for new construction.

Evans   This relates to the topic of environmental sustainability. LEED guidelines are too costly and unrealistic for the poor. I'd rather have a unit that is livable than having geothermal heat. Carbon neutral goals are good but unrealistic.

Burnham   All the guidelines are online at the BC Housing website, and one of our jobs is to try to push them out of shape. Architects have to be trained on what the users need. Users have to be understood

	and their issues respected. User input should be integrated into the actual building and planning of the site right from the get-go. The multiple challenges that users represent and will be facing have to be understood by the architects. Don't do cookie cutter design, customize for the specific needs of different user-groups.
Abbott	We were figuring out how much to spend in a building with an architect, and he was very worried about whether the building would incorporate spandrel glass or not. Spandrel glass is quite expensive and I was more concerned with the type of kitchen and finishing we could use. A lot of education has to happen with the architects. I'm sure spandrel glass would have been beautiful, but there are things that are far more important.
Bateman	From my experience working on the development of Bridge Housing a lot of solutions are deemed to be too expensive by bureaucrats when they are actually good solutions. We were told not to do a lot of things up front because of cost issues, and if we had done them we would have saved money in the long run. Higher cost elements are sometimes less expensive to maintain.
McBride	**In regards to the Southeast False Creek social housing units, some people are complaining about costs. What are your thoughts?**
Abbott	Because of the LEED Gold and LEED Platinum standards and carbon-neutral requirements, there's a ton of costs that have nothing to do with social housing. These environmental standards create a premium that would exist regardless of the buildings' uses. However, none of that gets mentioned, as the press just talks about the total cost.
Bailey	**How do you see gentrification changing social housing dynamics in the Downtown Eastside?**
Evans	People don't come to live in the Downtown Eastside to get services, but because it's one of the only places where people living on welfare can afford housing. It has been this way for years and years. The type of people who live in housing at the welfare rate of $375/month has changed a lot over the last thirty years. It used to be seasonal workers, people who worked at the docks,

and loggers, but now more of the people needing this housing in our community are people who have drug addictions, work in survival sex work, or are homeless. There has been a change in demographic patterns. It's a historically low income community and we've slowed down building social housing projects and have never built enough.

Burnham From 1993 there's been a real decline in the creation of social housing. In British Columbia it used to be 1,800 new units per year, but it went down to 600 in 1993. So you're looking at a loss of 1,200/yr for sixteen years. The decline has been worse for most other provinces across Canada.

Evans It's not rocket science. If we had continued to build, we would not be in this situation today.

Abbott It bothers me when people say that all neighbourhoods have to look the same. The Downtown Eastside has historically been a low income neighbourhood. Every city has a low income neighbourhood. It is not about the low income, it's about how you plan it and about how people live in it. The Downtown Eastside is a great community to live in. When I hear words like 'tragedy' and 'loss,' I disagree. It is not tragic, it is not broken, it is a community of people who live together and struggle with a number of issues. It is what it is. People are not just drug addicts and sex workers, but real people like anyone else.

Evans I can't stand when these people come from the States and find the Downtown Eastside horrible. Have you driven around Chicago? There are people living in boarded up buildings for miles and miles. What about Los Angeles? We have one tiny area and we are trying to get things done for the people for whom this community is home—things that will improve the stability of the neighbourhood for everyone, such as a safe injection site, food, and housing. We are actually thinking about the social problems here. In other cities, they are pushing people to the perimeter and out of sight, building condos, and destroying entire communities.

The studies about the creative class that have been coming out of the University of Toronto demonstrate that in economic environments where creativity is successfully celebrated, lower income and diversity is incorporated. Inclusivity creates productivity, not the contrary. Keeping lower income people out will not make things more productive.

Soules	**I want to know more about what happens when you sit down with your architects. What do you ask of them?**
Abbott	Security is a huge issue for all three of us. Finishes are also. We essentially have similar expectations around finishes. We want housing that doesn't look institutional from either the inside or the outside. We all want enough amenity spaces so there are opportunities for people to gather and create community. Water fountains are nice. I'd like more water features.
Burnham	I'd like to have more green space outside, such as spaces for gardens, which we don't get very often because of the density of the city.
Abbott	Space for place-based employment would be fabulous.
Evans	When we hired Arthur Erickson to design a purpose built building, he asked us to produce a series of bubble diagrams. We gave him a huge document with 100 pages of "in the perfect world, this is what we need." These ideas were generated by focus groups with residents and staff. The architects then spent two weeks in the hotel lobby, talking to residents about what they would like to see in their new home.
Burnham	We did a similar process for our project at Seymour Street and Davie Street to figure out the relationships between different spatial functions of the building.
Abbott	Atira is different from Portland and Coast, in part, because we work with children as well as adults. Our child-friendly spaces have different requirements, from the finishes to the colours. Colours are very important in child-friendly spaces. We need places for toys and play areas. And safety considerations like making sure that kids are not going to be able to grab kettles of coffee and burn themselves are vital. We use design charettes as a critical part of

the design process. Design consultants including architects tend to feel that they are in charge of everything, and there's some education that has to happen around that phenomena.

Hoff **Can you talk more explicitly about the benefits of your housing for residents?**

Burnham We did a sneak preview of a building at Robson Street and Richards Street last year. We drew numbers in a lottery to select tenants. When the future tenants walked into their own units, tears were streaming down. Just the joy of that experience is so amazing that it charges you up! And after getting housed, the residents walk differently; they are in charge of their lives.

Evans Some people are hard to recognize after they have been put into social housing. After shifting from sleeping on the street to having autonomy over their lives, the difference can be profound.

Abbott It is not just the housing that makes all the difference, but a number of benefits that come with it. Housing first, definitely. But people also need to have food, medical attention, community, and people to watch over them to see if they are well when they come home at night. All of these pieces are absolutely critical as well.

Burnham One thing we did that I found very powerful, for me and also for the architects, was to bring a focus group of tenants together. We all met to hear directly from the tenants what works for them and what they hold as valuable. This was very powerful for the architects to understand and get a sense of what is really important in the design.

Abbott Being able to have a voice is very powerful. Being involved in the process is so incredibly empowering for folks.

McBride **On the issue of social housing projects in middle-class communities and the fear of the poor, what are the ways to dissipate those fears and worries?**

Burnham There's a group called NIABY, "not in anyone's back yard"— just visit www.niaby.com—it's quite outrageous. They are using facts but in an interesting way. Our site for a future building in the Dunbar neighbourhood is at their ground zero. When faced with this type of opposition you have to be very patient. We took community members on tours of our facilities. We went through a process of identifying their fears. The best way is to meet with people one-on-one. This is the best way to deal with stigma. Facts don't do it; it has to be on a real personal level.

Abbott   We've had very different experiences depending on the type of housing we're building. Transition housing for women usually is well accepted as long as you don't talk about ongoing drug use. When sex work and drug use are put on the table there are issues. When we don't discuss these aspects the neighbours are happy to have us there.

In terms of larger societal prejudice, education has to happen from childhood onward. It's about compassion.

Evans   There's always the economic argument that tends to be successful. There's a lot of literature on how the cost of social housing is less than the cost of homelessness to society. This is a basic argument that is usually effective. Beyond that it is a compassion issue. What kind of society do we want to live in?

DESIGNING FOR AND WITH THE HOMELESS
COLLABORATIVE PROCESS IN DESIGN
REBECCA B. BATEMAN

A person without a fixed abode is viewed with suspicion in our society, labeled 'vagrant,' 'hobo,' [or] 'street person.' The lack of a home address can be a serious impediment to someone seeking a job, renting a place to live, or trying to vote. Those of us lucky enough to have a home may rarely reflect on our good fortune.[1]

Homelessness does not equate to hopelessness, nor does the state of being homeless or inadequately housed mean that people lack the capacity to participate in the design of their own housing. This paper will examine two examples of successful housing projects in which those to be housed have been active collaborators in designing their own homes, drawing out crucial lessons for architects interested in the development of social housing. The paper will also examine an innovative collaborative methodology in which architects set aside the role of 'expert' to take on the role of social activists within communities. The primary objective of the paper is to identify best practices in collaborative design that can be implemented in the development of social housing.

Society tends to define the homeless by what they are not and by what they do not have. As a result, they are often infantilized by a society that views them as either lazy con-artists living off the largesse of taxpayer-financed welfare programs or as the unfortunate and pitiable victims of greater political and economic forces or personal tragedy.[2] By emphasizing certain aspects of individuals' existence and imputing to it a limiting set of moral characteristics—helplessness, shiftlessness, worthlessness—a form of symbolic violence is added to the physical and social violence already experienced by homeless people.[3] Within this frame of reference, the homeless are seen as having little competence or ability to help work towards solutions that address homelessness.[4]

The design of social housing, not unlike most architecture, but especially so for housing for the homeless, is scrutinized in terms of its finished product—is it well designed? Does it serve the needs of those who live and work there? Does it respond to the surrounding built environment in a manner that doesn't stigmatize the residents or aggravate the neighbours? Did it come in on budget? Is it a good example of taxpayer dollars well spent? These are all valuable and important questions. What usually doesn't receive that same level of consideration, however, is by what process did a particular building come into existence? In searching for innovative ways to address homelessness through built form, it is also important to consider innovative participatory and collaborative processes that include the end-users in meaningful ways in the conception, design, and sometimes even in the construction, of their future homes.

What if homeless people are viewed as having community? Sociologist David Wagner poses this provocative question in his study of the pseudonymous homeless community of Checkerboard Square. He points out that the structure of both private markets and the public sector forces homeless people to present themselves as autonomous "atomized biographies," and to separate themselves from their broader group in order to access the resources (social assistance, housing, etc.) that are necessary for survival.[5] This process of individuation works against and denies the existence of any sense of belonging or community that homeless individuals may have formed. What if, Wagner asks, "the dense social networks and cohesive subcultures that constitute the homeless community were utilized by advocates, social workers, and others?"[6] And what if architects and nonprofit housing developers were among the 'others'? What might the results look like?

They might look very much like two housing projects in Toronto: StreetCity, built in 1989, and Strachan House, built in 1996 (often called StreetCity II). Both projects involved homeless persons in the design development process and produced innovative housing that reflects residents' ideas about what constitutes safety and 'home,' and that uses the street—a place of socialization, tolerance, and community, as well as danger—as a central design element.

StreetCity's genesis began when a group of homeless and formerly homeless men and hostel workers who were recently dislodged from a closed hostel self-organized and approached a Toronto housing provider, the Homes First Society, with an idea for a new housing project. 'The Balcony Bunch,' as this group called themselves, proposed an alternative form of shelter in which people could experience the stability and privacy of permanent housing in a way that would enable them to assume the responsibilities of tenancy within a supportive environment. The Balcony Bunch named their vision StreetCity and along with Homes First was successful in attracting government support. The City of Toronto supplied a 24,000 ft^2 former Canada Post maintenance garage and various levels of provincial, metropolitan, and municipal governments offered approximately half a million dollars for capital costs.[7] Architects Marie Black and Walter Moffat were tasked with renovating the large, open, and single story interior into housing that reflected the Balcony Bunch's desire for a heightened sense of community.[8] The result was a unique housing environment, conceived as temporary, that operated in Toronto until 2003.

A wide, internal corridor, called Main Street by residents, ran the entire length of the building and directly under a pre-existing central skylight. This space served as a gathering place for communal meals and meetings as well as functioning as circulation. On either side of Main Street there were six separate structures, three for men and three for women, each containing twelve individual private bedrooms with a bed, dresser, chair, and small refrigerator. Each structure, or 'house,' included a shared kitchen, washrooms, and a lounge area. The lounge areas were designed as courtyards that adjoined Main Street and led to the part of the house containing the bedrooms.

The largest portion of StreetCity's floor area was dedicated to shared and semi-shared spaces within which private space was situated. Much of the space in StreetCity was not specifically programmed, resulting in negotiable space that the community could use as it saw fit.[9]

StreetCity operated twelve years longer than originally planned and was a considerable success. The project, however, was by no means perfect. Interest and participation in its self-governance declined over the years of its operation. Women often felt less comfortable in the male-designed facility. The 'wet' philosophy, which allowed drug and alcohol use by residents (though not on Main Street), resulted in significant stress and pressure on staff as they dealt with frequent disputes and violent behaviour among residents. Local media sensationalized StreetCity as nothing more than a brothel and a haven for drug dealers.[10]

But the lessons of StreetCity—that homeless people can take an active role in both the design and the management of their housing; that for many people, housing needs to be both community and shelter; and that shelter that is flexible enough to accommodate both transitional stays and permanent residents is a valuable form of housing—informed the development of a second StreetCity, Strachan House, that continues to serve the needs of the homeless people of Toronto. In 1995, the City of Toronto donated a 40,000 ft^2 former lumber warehouse to Homes First, along with a $500,000 capital grant, to build Strachan House, a second-generation and more permanent StreetCity.[11] Levitt Goodman Architects were hired to design the $3.3 million transformation.

The Homes First philosophy is that any monies intended for housing the homeless belong not to the housing society, but to the homeless themselves. In keeping with this ethical position, the end-users of Strachan House— residents as well as staff—were involved in its design. The design process took six years and involved the architects attending group discussions at city drop-in centres, meeting with front-line workers, and incorporating the input and feedback gathered through ongoing design meetings with residents and staff.[12] Janna Levitt states that her firm's intention was to "treat homeless people like we would treat any other client" and that the design process was "as much a community-building exercise as it was a building exercise."[13] The approach was considered highly unorthodox—consulting the homeless was simply not done.

To facilitate community consultations Homes First created a group that included social scientists, social service agency personnel, and front-line workers as well as the architects. This group approached people where they lived, whether in shelters or on the streets, and asked them what they would like if they lived in housing, and what they would need in order to be able to come in off the street. Through this process terms such as 'living room' and 'dining room' were rejected as being class and gender biased. As Ms. Levitt states:

> Here, there weren't the same kinds of rules. In fact, we had to throw out all the rules. This project had to work for the people living here. You can't just talk about living rooms or dining rooms because that implies a certain way of living that might not jell with the way these people want to live. [14]

This prompted the architects to reconsider the character of domestic space. "Because a lot of the residents didn't have the language to describe what they needed in a residence," Ms. Levitt recalls, "some of them actually acted out their needs and the ways in which certain crisis situations might occur. And we carefully measured and codified these demonstrations, so that the design process really became a sort of choreography."[15]

Like StreetCity, Strachan House is a 'city within a city.' The building is organized into autonomous 'houses' that incorporate private individual rooms along with shared kitchens and bathrooms. Circulation corridors link the houses and open out into informal common areas. A 'town hall' provides a central gathering place for residents. Strachan House offers a range of ways to inhabit it—residents can live in their private rooms or choose to 'camp out'

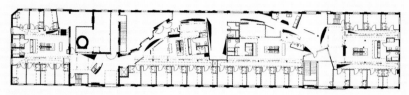

3RD FLOOR

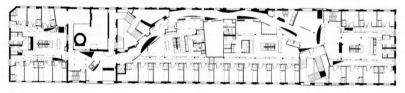

2ND FLOOR

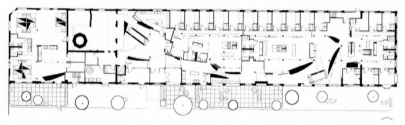

GROUND FLOOR

Strachan House, Levitt Goodman Architects, Toronto, Canada, 1999.
Photographs and plans by Levitt Goodman Architects.

in some of the open and undefined spaces. Doors to individual rooms can of course be closed and locked but are coupled with windows that look out into the shared space, thereby offering residents the ability to maintain security and privacy while still connecting to the larger community. Artists integrated found objects and glass into varied patterns in the poured concrete floors, successfully integrating art with function and contributing to the building's sense of place.[16]

Levitt Goodman Architects were awarded the Governor-General's Medal of Excellence in Architecture for Strachan House. As Ms. Levitt recalls, winning the award was especially important since the local architectural community regarded Strachan House as "a total yawn" prior to external validation of the building's design excellence. "Strachan House still isn't regarded [by the mainstream architectural profession] as being great architecture. That is the biggest challenge for the education system for architects—to dispel the notion that designing non-profit housing is a form of charity or social work, rather than 'real' architecture."[17]

StreetCity and Strachan House afforded homeless people an opportunity to actively participate in the design and management of their own housing. In both cases, homeless men and women were even involved in the construction—each was designed to enable this involvement by intentionally designing parts of the building so they could be constructed by people with low-level skills.[18] And in both cases, the resulting design broke with previous conventions regarding the ratio of public to private space, and notions of transitional versus permanent housing, and 'home' versus the street.

Seeking out potential end-users on the streets and in shelters was not usual practice for architects. This was radical and ground-breaking work that was not supported by many in the profession. Since the early 1990s, however, a number of organizations and design centres have been established whose specific mandate is to collaborate with marginalized and underprivileged communities to bring good design to people who are seldom able to benefit from the skills and expertise of architects and other design professionals. All operate from a philosophy that the architectural profession should be socially conscious and that social activism is an appropriate and important role for architects, but not all define their role in quite the same way, or emphasize process to the same extent.

Collaboration, in the sense of these alternative practices, can be defined in a number of different ways. For some, collaboration is a form of community service, a departure from standard architectural practice, and a means by which participants can engage in service learning and experience the effects of poverty, racism, marginalization, and dispossession. Others reject a service-oriented model for one that is unapologetically and intentionally political, that works to create positive social change, that seeks to overturn the relations of power through the creation of literacy and the exchange of knowledge—and that produces good design.

Four of the most prominent and well-established programs in community-based collaborative architecture are the Detroit Collaborative Design Center, the Miami University Design/Build Studio and Center for Community Engagement, Design Corps, and Auburn University's Rural Studio. These four sit roughly along a continuum from more radically engaged collaboration to service-oriented collaboration. The Detroit Collaborative Design Center (DCDC) offers perhaps the most poignant example of radically engaged collaboration while Rural Studio is an excellent standard of service-oriented collaboration.

The DCDC was established in 1993 at the University of Detroit Mercy School of Architecture and involves architecture students in a program of real-life design projects for exclusively non-profit organizations. Dan Pitera, DCDC's director, calls the Center's work an architecture of praxis, as opposed to practice. This entails consciously political actions that aim to create a more equitable and just society by "amplifying the diminished voice" of those who have been marginalized and dehumanized. An architecture of praxis, in this sense, aims to encourage and support self-determination among those who have been subjected to a long history of discrimination and tutelage.

The DCDC rejects the concept of 'service,' with its implication of a hierarchical relationship between giver and receiver, in favour of 'engagement'; a more equitable partnership among participants. Towards this end, the Center employs a capacity building and literacy-creating process, one that challenges the myths about participatory community design—that it costs too much, that ordinary people cannot participate because they lack expert knowledge, and that participation compromises design quality. The DCDC recognizes and promotes the political consequences of the projects it undertakes.[19]

The DCDC's typical approach incorporates a series of seven workshops that include all stakeholders to define project goals and set objectives; establish programmatic criteria; establish visual criteria; establish a quality model; review program space requirements and set budget goals; determine the conceptual arrangement of spaces; and confirm the final design and budget. The process builds design literacy in participants by "celebrating everyday experience." Staff and students at the DCDC help demystify architectural terminology and concepts, teach people to understand architectural drawings, and take stakeholders on tours of buildings to identify the various ways that design issues can be addressed.[20]

Design collaboration that seeks to create heightened literacy and transform the distribution of power and knowledge in society requires operating from a philosophy that envisions architecture's role as not just service provision, but as directly helping to effect that transformation in ways that extend beyond built form. This is a process with an intention not just to draw on local knowledge, but to build community capacity and leave a lasting legacy that is in addition to the building itself. This approach to design is particularly appropriate when working with the marginalized and the non-profit societies that work for and with them.

So how to put highly collaborative architecture as exemplified by the DCDC into increased practice in the design of social housing? The standard approach in most jurisdictions, including British Columbia, involves very little collaboration with end-users. Architects with backgrounds and experience in the design of social housing work closely with clients—the housing providers—but their contact with the potential residents is often minimal and short-lived. Programming decisions are made by housing providers with guidance from development consultants and in close collaboration with the primary funder. The housing providers know their client's housing and services needs well. But, as architect Gregory Henriquez comments: "working directly with the future residents of a project, rather than only with the housing provider, can result in a more respectful design. People are looking not just for a place to live, but also for more control over their lives and environment, and their futures."[21] Intensely collaborative design will only find wider use if its benefits are made clear.

Perhaps the biggest obstacle is related to cost. Common perception is that a highly collaborative process will unnecessarily add to cost. While a higher up-front cost is undoubtedly involved, it is possible that overall cost-savings can be achieved by better connecting design and programming with residents' needs. The process can result in a more appropriate, more efficient, and more cost-effective building. Also, residents that have been involved in the design process typically have more pride in their home, which translates into less wear-and-tear and reduced maintenance costs. In addition to life-cycle cost-saving, a highly collaborative process can result in more innovative and outstanding architecture as the approach works to overcome the deficiencies in the status quo. Beyond the possibilities for better and less-costly buildings, there are the value–added benefits of community capacity and literacy building.

Through collaborative design that draws upon the knowledge, experience, and expertise of people in need of housing—especially those who have experienced absolute homelessness and have lived on the street—architects can participate in counteracting the view of the homeless as lacking in agency and competence. The result can be buildings that better meet the needs of residents, not as defined by 'experts,' but by the residents themselves. The architectural profession can become a more "participatory practice, one that engages diversity of thought, action, and collectivity from both within and without."[22]

To commit to an architecture of collaborative praxis is to express a strong belief in the importance and power of a utopian vision of society. As architects José Gámez and Susan Rogers have written:

> [W]e have to reconceive utopianism not so much as a practice but as a process, one that has the potential to transform both the production of space and the distribution of social and political power. This concept moves architecture beyond a solely physical practice and redefines academic and professional architecture as fields that envision alternative futures and have the means to help realize them.[23]

With collaborative praxis, architecture can perhaps help society move toward the alternative future in which those unfortunate enough to be homeless are treated as competent, thoughtful, and as holding part of the key to the utopia in which everyone is adequately housed.

1. Clare Copper Marcus, *House As a Mirror of Self: Exploring the Deeper Meaning of Home* (Berkeley: Conari Press, 1995), 4.
2. Rae Bridgman, "The Architecture of Homelessness and Utopian Pragmatics" in *Utopian Studies* 9.1 (1998): 52.
3. Greg Marston, "Constructing the Meaning of Social Exclusion as a Policy Metaphor" in *Social Constructionism in Housing Research*, ed. Keith Jacobs, Jim Kemeny and Tony Manzi (Burlington: Ashgate, 2004), 88.
4. Bridgman, "The Architecture of Homelessness," 52.
5. David Wagner, *Checkerboard Square: Culture and Resistance in a Homeless Community* (Boulder: Westview, 1993), 179.
6. Ibid, 180.
7. Rae Bridgman, *StreetCities: Rehousing the Homeless* (Peterborough: Broadview, 2006), 103–106; Paul Dowling, "StreetCity" in *Documentation of Best Practices Addressing Homelessness* (Ottawa: Canada Mortgage and Housing Corporation, 1999), 86.
8. Bridgman, *StreetCities*, 74–75.
9. Bridgman, *StreetCities*, 108–109; Dowling, "StreetCity," 75–76.
10. Bridgman, *StreetCities*, 139; Dowling, "StreetCity," 77.
11. Bridgman, *StreetCities*, 140.
12. Janna Levitt, personal communication March 21, 2009.
13. Ibid.
14. Dowling, "StreetCity," 78.
15. Bridgman, *StreetCities*, 139–151.
16. Levitt, personal communication, paraphrased.
17. Ibid.
18. Leonie Sandercock, "The Difference That Theory Makes" in *Towards Cosmopolis: Planning for Multicultural Cities* (Chichester: Wiley, 1998), 85–104.
19. *Detroit Collaborative Design Center: Amplifying the Diminished Voice* directed by Sheri Blake (Winnipeg: Sou International Ltd, 2006), DVD.
20. Ibid.
21. Gregory Henriquez. In-class presentation for ARCH 544b at the School of Architecture and Landscape Architecture, University of British Columbia, March 9, 2009.
22. José L. Gámez and Susan Rogers, "An Architecture of Change" in *Expanding Architecture: Design as Activism*, ed. Bryan Bell and Katie Wakeford (New York: Metropolis, 2008), 24.
23. Ibid, 23.

PARTICIPANTS

Seminar Students

Students enrolled in *The Architecture of Social Housing: Ideas, Actions, and Futures*, taught at the UBC School of Architecture and Landscape Architecture, Spring 2009:

Magali Bailey

Rebecca Bateman

Bryan Beça

Maranatha Coulas

Stephanie da Silva

Idette de Boer

Anya Georgivejic

Andrea Hoff

Meghan McBride

Rodrigo Ferrari Nunes

Matt Purvis

Seminar Guests

Guest speakers for *The Architecture of Social Housing: Ideas, Actions, and Futures*:

Janice Abbott. Executive Director, Atira Women's Resource Society.

Darrell Burnham. Executive Director, Coast Foundation Society.

Karen Cooper. BC Housing.

Craig Crawford. Vice President of Development Services, BC Housing.

Earl Crow. Resident of the Pennsylvania Hotel, a building
    operated by Portland Hotel Society.

Liz Evans. Executive Director, Portland Hotel Society.

Judy Graves. Outreach Worker, City of Vancouver.

Cameron Gray. Managing Director, Social Development, City of Vancouver.

Gregory Henriquez, MAIBC. Managing Partner, Henriquez Partners Architects.

Stephanie Illesca. Resident of Crossroads, a building
    operated by Coast Foundation Society.

Dane Jansen, MAIBC. Principal, DYS Architecture.

Stuart Lyon, MAIBC. Principal, GBL Architecture.

Jim O'Dea. Principal, Terra Housing Consultants.

Patrick Stewart, MAIBC. Principal, Patrick Stewart Architect.

Karen Stone. Executive Director, BC Non-Profit Housing Association.

Marcel Swayne. Executive Director, Lu'ma Native Housing Society.

Stuart Thomas. Principal, Terra Housing Consultants.

Competitors

Entrants in the Future Social design competition:

Carole Alexander, Tyler Best & Veronica Robertson

Emma Artis, Lauren Macaulay & Angelique Pilon

Caitlan Bailey & Magali Bailey

Matthew Beall

Amber Bruce, Sophie MacNeill & Morgan Wallace

Stewart Burgess

Aidan Carruthers, Federica Piccone & Elsa Snyder

Maranatha Coulas & Meghan McBride

Brooke Dedrick, Courtney Healey & Chris Sklar

Ashley Gilbert & Alicia Medina

Kali Gordon & Amy Oliver

Jonathan Griffiths & Baktash Ilbeiggi

Mehdi Hashemi & Scott Keck

Daniel Irvine, Elizabeth Laing & Ariel Mieling

Joshua Jordan & Phil Riley

Christian Kliegel & Katy Young

Jon-Scott Kohli & Alex Manson

Jordan Lock

Sara Morgan & David Paterson

Matt Purvis

Jonathan Yu & Donald Zhou

Jury

Jury for the Future Social design competition:

Jury Chair

Matthew Soules MAIBC. Director, Matthew Soules Architecture
and Assistant Professor, School of Architecture and
Landscape Architecture, UBC (non-voting).

Jurors

Craig Crawford. Vice President of Development Services, BC Housing.

Liz Evans. Executive Director, Portland Hotel Society.

Bruce Haden, MAIBC. Principal, Hotson Bakker Boniface Haden.

George Wagner. Professor and Chair of Architecture, School of
Architecture and Landscape Architecture, UBC.

First published in 2012 by BLUE*IMPRINT*

Text and images © 2012 the Contributors

All rights reserved. No part of this publication may be reproduced, stored in a retrieval system or transmitted, in any form or by any means, electronic, mechanic, photocopying, recording or otherwise, without the written permission of the publisher. The publisher does not have control over and does not assume any responsibility for author or third-party websites or their content.

Library and Archives Canada Cataloguing in Publication
   Future social / edited by Matthew Soules.

Includes index.
ISBN 978-1-897476-30-7

   1. Architecture, Domestic—Social aspects—British Columbia—Vancouver.
   2. Architecture and society—British Columbia—Vancouver.
   3. Homeless persons—Housing—British Columbia—Downtown-Eastside (Vancouver).
   4. Housing—British Columbia—Vancouver. I. Soules, Matthew II. Title.

NA2543.S6F88 2011   720.1'03   C2010-905670-1

Edited by Matthew Soules
Designed by Bryan Lemos Beça

Printed in China.

We gratefully acknowledge the support of the Ministry of Housing and Social Development on behalf of the Province of British Columbia, and the University of British Columbia School of Architecture + Landscape Architecture. Thanks also to the gracious presenters who generously donated their time and energy into helping us understand.

We gratefully acknowledge for their financial support of our publishing program the Canada Council for the Arts, the BC Arts Council, and the Government of Canada through the Canada Book Fund (CBF).

The views expressed in this publication are solely those of the author(s). The Ministry of Housing and Social Development and the Government of British Columbia do not necessarily share, support, nor endorse those views.

University of British Columbia
School of Architecture + Landscape Architecture
402–6333 Memorial Road, Vancouver, BC V6T 1Z2
www.sala.ubc.ca

FUTURE SOCIAL